A PENGUIN SPECIAL

s165

TWENTIETH CENTURY SOCIALISM

SOCIALIST UNION

TWENTIETH CENTURY SOCIALISM

THE ECONOMY OF TO-MORROW

by Socialist Union

PENGUIN BOOKS

Penguin Books Ltd, Harmondsworth, Middlesex

U.S.A.: Penguin Books Inc., 3300 Clipper Mill Road, Baltimore 11, Md

CANADA: Penguin Books (Canada) Ltd, 178 Norseman Street,
Toronto 18, Ontario

AUSTRALIA: Penguin Books Pty Ltd, 762 Whitehorse Road,
Mitcham, Victoria

SOUTH AFRICA: Penguin Books (S.A.) Pty Ltd, Gibraltar House,
Regent Road, Sea Point, Cape Town

—

Published in Penguin Books 1956

Made and printed in Great Britain
by Wyman & Sons Ltd
London, Reading, and Fakenham

CONTENTS

FOREWORD

TO THE READER

Please do not seek in this book what you cannot find. There are many different ways of writing about socialism, and we have chosen only one. Imaginative writers have painted an artist's picture of life lived differently in the socialist society of their dreams. Sober historians have traced the varying strands in the development of socialist thought and practice. Political theorists have drawn up constitutions for the socialist commonwealth of the future. Economists have discussed how a socialist economy would work. Not least, there have been the many programmes in which socialist parties have said what they would do if given power.

Our book does not fit into any of these categories. It is neither prophecy nor history; it is not an essay in political or economic theory; and it certainly lays no claim to be an election manifesto. It is, rather, a study in applied ethics – socialist ethics applied to the sphere of economic organization. We share Keir Hardie's view that socialism is 'at bottom a question of ethics or morals. It has mainly to do with the relationships which should exist between a man and his fellows'. Our aim has been to find a comprehensive and consistent view of the socialist economy of to-morrow, which combines the idealism inherent in our conception of the good society with the realism essential to bring it about.

True, we deal only with domestic economic organization. All the many problems of external economic relations, of trade and aid as between nations, have been excluded. Not that we underestimate their importance, particularly for a small country like Britain which yet has vast overseas responsibilities, combined with a peculiar economic vulnerability of her own; nor do we in any way underrate the obligations of socialists to help those in the underdeveloped areas of the world, who are less wealthy than ourselves. But our prime concern in this book was more limited – to work out what socialism could mean in the economy of any one nation. We have taken Britain as the example, but the principles which we put forward have a more general application. They can be helpful, we believe, to socialists everywhere.

The discussions which laid the foundations of this book began among a group of our members, but each draft was discussed by the membership as a whole, so as to reach the greatest possible measure of agreement. Much valuable advice was given by several distinguished experts to whom we would like to record our thanks. The task of elaborating all these views into a coherent argument, and the actual drafting, was entrusted to Allan Flanders, Senior Lecturer in Industrial Relations at the University of Oxford, and Rita Hinden, Editor of *Socialist Commentary*.

We are well aware that what we have to say is not the last word on this subject. But we offer it to our fellow-socialists as an honest attempt to think out afresh the foundations of a socialist faith and its implications in the modern world. It will not, we think, be without its appeal to all men and women who reject that view, so rife to-day, which takes material betterment as the sole measure of economic progress.

February 1956

SOCIALIST UNION
447 Strand,
London w.c.2

'A great principle may be so overlain by dogmatic interpretation as to be unrecognizable; nay, the dogma may in course of time come to be considered of greater importance than the principle itself. It is well, therefore, to examine all formulas and phrases which we are told are not only part and parcel of the true doctrine, but the only real interpretation thereof.'

J. KEIR HARDIE in the *Labour Leader*, 1904

Introduction

I

A RECKONING WITH THE PAST

The socialist movement was cradled in the conditions of nineteenth century capitalism. It was an expression of revolt against an economic system which combined unparalleled material progress with appalling human misery. The English social scene towards the close of the century was painted in the unforgettable words of Robert Blatchford:

Go out into the streets of any big English town, and use your eyes, John. What do you find? You find some rich and idle, wasting unearned wealth to their own shame and injury and the shame and injury of others. You find hard-working people packed away in vile unhealthy streets. You find little children famished, dirty, and half naked outside the luxurious clubs, shops, hotels, and theatres. You find men and women overworked and underpaid. You find vice and want and disease cheek by jowl with religion and culture and wealth. ...
This is not rhetoric, it is hard fact ... I say that wrong and sorrow are here crushing the life out of our brothers and sisters. I say that you, in common with all men, are responsible for the things that are. I say that it is your duty to seek the remedy; and I say that if you seek it you will find it.*

This and many another clarion call to action did not go unheeded. An increasing number of people, who were proud to be known as socialists, refused to accept the hard facts around them as inevitable and ordained. They took it upon themselves to seek the remedy. Although differing in their views on the exact shape of things to come, on their central message they were united – the economic system in being

* Robert Blatchford, *Merrie England*, 1908 ed., p. 251.

was wrong and had to be replaced by another and totally different one. Minor reforms to ease the sufferings of the victims of capitalism were all very well, but what was wanted was a new system which would have no victims at all. In setting this as their goal, socialists distinguished themselves from all other reform movements of the time.

Two Opposing Systems

On one point only did they agree with the defenders of the established order. They shared with them the idea of there being two, distinct, opposing and ultimately irreconcilable economic systems – capitalism and socialism. You could have the one or replace it by the other, but you could not mix the two. Each party sought to give theoretical backing to the system it supported. In keeping with the spirit of the time, allegedly scientific theories were developed – on the one hand to prove the inevitability and the essential goodness of capitalism; on the other to prove the same about socialism.

The defenders of capitalism drew support from the new and growing science of economics. All economic processes, they claimed, were regulated by the laws of supply and demand. The proper role of government was to hold the ring for free competition under which these laws could have full play. Wages and prices, rents and profits were then fixed by the impersonal, and therefore impartial, mechanism of the market. What could be better than equality before the law in economic as in political life?

What was more, the system was such that, as Adam Smith had said, 'every individual ... is led by an invisible hand to promote an end which was no part of his intention' – the common good. Personal gain might be the spur to enterprise and hard work, but the pressure of competition kept prices down so that everyone could reap the benefits of rising production. True, some people were lucky and some unlucky; there were those who could live on their wealth without noticeably displaying enterprise, and those who landed on the scrap-heap of the poor law with no opportunity to work at all. This was unfortunate; but the consolation could be found outside the realm of economics. It gave the rich the opportunity to practise charity and the poor, resignation. Extremes of success and failure were part of the natural lot of man.

Socialists regarded this kind of theorizing with much the same abhorrence as they regarded capitalism itself. To them it was a rationalization of what they knew, by its fruits, to be bad. Without hesitation, they challenged all its assumptions. Why should the means of production be left in private hands, they asked? Why should there be a free market when it led to such galling inequalities? Was there really no spur to effort and material progress other than the lure of personal gain? To all these questions they found answers in the vision of a socialist system – a system which would replace private by public ownership, the free market by a regulated economy, and the profit motive by a spirit of service to the community. The socialist system to come was seen in terms of direct opposites to the hated system in being.

The socialist conception, no less than the capitalist, had to be backed by theory, a theory as scientific as that of orthodox economics. The unbending laws of supply and demand were opposed by the equally unbending laws of social change. The capitalists, so socialists asserted, had failed to grasp that the very mechanism of the market would bring about its own breakdown and its replacement by a socialist system. For free competition, instead of remaining free, stimulated the capitalists themselves to create monopolies, while the workers were forced, by the stern logic of the labour market, to organize their own strength in self-protection. The growth of large-scale industries would ease – indeed it would positively invite – their final transfer to public ownership. Even the automatic market adjustments could not prevent recurring and deepening crises, and their disastrous effects would, in the end, shake the tottering system to its ruin. This theory, that the dynamic laws governing the development of capitalism made the coming of socialism inevitable, was expounded most systematically in the works of Marx and Engels, but in some degree it permeated every shade of socialist thought.

The irreconcilability of capitalism and socialism, conceived as two rival economic systems, thus became an assumption which was widely shared by capitalists and socialists alike. A capitalist, if he had not been corrupted by socialist propaganda, was an unrelenting champion of private enterprise, the free market and the profit motive. A socialist was irrevocably opposed to each of these. In theory, at least, there could be no enduring half-way house; socialism was the direct antithesis to *laissez faire* capitalism. This simple conception, which once dominated socialist thought, has undoubtedly faded with the passing of time, and the theories which supported it have been sharply challenged by events, yet its influence is by no means exhausted. Like a ghost from the past it still haunts our thinking. The time has surely come to give what is dead a decent burial.

The Breakdown of Theory

For what are the facts? The capitalist system, even in the heyday of *laissez faire*, never coincided with the theoretical model of orthodox economics. There never was a time when the market was really free and competition gave everyone an opportunity to grow rich. With the passage of the years, capitalism has continued to diverge in practice from what it was held to be in theory. Its own inner dynamic and increasing democratic pressures have changed it – at least in its British version – almost out of recognition. Every one of its earlier institutions has in some way been modified. If what we have now is still called 'capitalism' on the ground that much capital remains privately owned, then the old genus has produced a strange new species.

The traditional theories of socialists have fared no better. The forecast that capitalism was not a static system has proved correct enough, but confident prophecies about its collapse and inevitable replacement by socialism now ring strangely false. Where revolutions have overthrown the regimes of the past and replaced them by their antithesis, the result has been to exchange new tyrannies for old. Private capitalists and landlords have been eliminated, but so have free labour movements. What once were regarded as inherently socialist institutions – public enterprise, a planned economy, even social services – are deliberately employed to reduce every individual to a helpless victim of the state. If communism is to be the result of creating a straight antithesis to the capitalist system, then clearly socialists want to think again.

But the greatest challenge to the old belief in the two opposing systems has come from the success of piecemeal reforms. Despite what was said in theory, in its practical politics the British labour movement has never accepted the view that capitalism could not be changed from within. If the capitalists have found it convenient to depart from their theoretical model, so have the socialists who wanted to do something more than talk about the future. Instead of waiting for the day when capitalism could be replaced in its entirety by socialism, they have taken action, and, step by step, some of the most pernicious evils of capitalism have been eradicated. Through the growth of collective bargaining, the introduction of social services, the constant extension of redistributive taxation, the spread of co-operative and municipal enterprise, and, most potent accomplishment of all, the coming of full employment, the lives of working people have been transformed, even though private capital survives and, indeed, still dominates our economy.

All these piecemeal changes are now woven into the very texture of our social fabric. The Welfare State, which is neither capitalism nor socialism, has been created. This was a development which no theory had bargained for. But whereas capitalists may find it expedient to accept the new *status quo*, even to acclaim it as their own invention, socialists are now divided and confused. The very success of their achievements seems to threaten the ground beneath their feet. Any belief that the workers could hope for nothing, except increasing misery, under capitalism has been destroyed with a completeness beyond argument. In its place a new anxiety has arisen – that in a society lulled into complacency by material comforts, the struggle for socialism will lose its old dynamic and, in the end, be abandoned. Obviously people can no longer be moved – as Blatchford moved them – by simple pictures of the horrors on their doorstep, for most of these horrors are no more.

The Present Dilemma

In this unexpected and perplexing situation diverging views were bound to be heard. At the one extreme there are some who resolutely refuse to come to terms with the facts. They dismiss all that has been won as a mere patching up of capitalism, which one day – they insist – will sink into its inevitable collapse. For them that final, shattering economic crisis is always round the corner. So they tilt at the old windmills and take refuge in the easy slogan that all that is still wrong would be righted if only we had a socialist system cut to the pattern of traditional belief. They are the confirmed doctrinaires of the movement. At the other extreme there are those who draw the conclusion that too much theory has already led the movement on to false paths. They see no need for further talk about economic systems. For them socialism has become nothing more than an exercise in social engineering. They are content to deal with immediate problems as they arise, providing socialists are permitted to be the leading firm of social engineers. They waste no time on ultimate objectives. They are the confirmed empiricists of the movement.

It is easy to-day to recognize these extreme viewpoints in the so-called left and right wings of the labour movement. They both fail to satisfy the majority of socialists. The first does not convince, the second does not inspire. Each can see the mote in the other's eyes, but both have lost their bearings. The doctrinaires are still using a map which is out of date; the empiricists no longer have a compass to guide them. Both are suffering from the breakdown of the conception of the two stereotyped antithetical systems, and the absence of any philosophical substitute appropriate to the mid-twentieth century.

Some new vision must now be sought. Without a comprehensive view of what it is they want to achieve, socialists cannot hope to create the will for social change. But – and this is the real lesson to be learnt from the destruction of the old theories – this comprehensive view cannot be found in an institutional blueprint for an economic system which will hold at all times and in all places. Socialism cannot be tied in this way to one rigid pattern of economic doctrine, void of meaning and relevance to the coming generation.

The ultimate source of the confusion and division which afflict socialism to-day is that its true ends are being forgotten. The doctrinaires have deified the means that were once thought to bring certain salvation, into ends in themselves. For them socialism is measured in terms of more public enterprise, more planning, more money spent on social services – irrespective of the results. The empiricists, on the other hand, in becoming more realistic about the choice of means, have scaled down their ends to nothing more than the immediately acceptable. In neither viewpoint is there any room for the ideals which have been the one enduring foundation of the socialist faith.

PART ONE

The Ends in View

2
A CONFLICT OF VALUES

At bottom the conflict between capitalism and socialism has always been a conflict of values. Capitalists have accepted material values as the main criterion of progress. What socialists have wanted to see embodied in the economy were the universal human ideals of equality, freedom and fellowship. These ideals all express in their various ways the basic worth of every human personality. They make man the measure of the good society. It is his equality, his freedom, his fellowship – not only his economic advantage – which have been the ends of socialist endeavour.*

For a century and more the emphasis in socialist propaganda has, it is true, been on redressing the balance between wealth and poverty, for there lay the most urgent need. But this demand was never rooted in the materialist philosophy on which capitalism thrived. From the start socialists have consistently protested against the vulgar view of life and society which – in the words of the *Communist Manifesto* – 'left no other nexus between man and man than naked self-interest' and 'drowned everything in the icy water of egotistical calculation'. The British socialist tradition, in particular, owes much to an ethical rejection of the crude and shameless materialism with which capitalism degraded the whole of social life.

No one who reads the writings of the early socialists can possibly doubt that it was the effect of capitalism on the lives of people – its denial of human values – which roused

* See *Socialism – A New Statement of Principles*. By Socialist Union, 1952.

their fiercest indignation and concern. They might criticize the capitalist system as being wasteful of resources, they might regard it as moving inevitably towards its decline, but what moved them to action was the avoidable suffering and misery it caused, its sacrifice of man to money.

The clash between capitalist and socialist values is as irreconcilable to-day as it has ever been. But it has become blurred through entanglement with the other, and seemingly parallel, conflict between the two stereotyped economic systems. As the theories woven around this second conflict have been shattered, so the deeper truth of the first tends also to be lost. Capital and labour are thought to be struggling over nothing more than the division of the product, whereas in fact two distinct and opposing conceptions of the nature and destiny of man are ranged against each other. Whatever may happen to economic systems, capitalism and socialism as social philosophies remain as fire and water; they do not mix.

To-day socialists are in danger of forgetting this simple starting-point to their philosophy. There is an inclination to accept the unspoken, capitalist assumption underlying so much of modern thought on economic organization – that it should be judged only by its economic results. And what are its economic results? They are the quantitative things which economists can measure statistically – output, trade, costs, incomes, everything that can be stated in material or monetary terms. The less tangible results of economic organization, what it does to the dignity of people or the quality of their lives, lie beyond their calculations – to be dismissed as irrelevant or simply ignored.

The arguments supporting this partial and distorted view of economic organization are far more seductive now than they were during the nineteenth century. No longer is the attempt made to identify private profit with the welfare of the nation. Instead, such acceptable aims as high productivity, national solvency, a rising standard of living, have become the familiar terms of reference. As no one in his senses can dispute their importance or their urgency, why not – so it is argued – concentrate on them as a united nation, rather than waste energy in futile controversy on the issues which divide us? So much thought has still to be given to the discovery of the best techniques and forms of organization to make our economy more efficient and viable, why complicate matters by introducing ethics into economics?

Yet where do these arguments lead? Once material are substituted for human values, the claims of socialism as a superior economic system become of doubtful validity. If increased production is to be the criterion, can we really prove that socialist policies will be more effective than the capitalist policies which set the pace in the United States to-day? Can we argue convincingly that greater equality of incomes or the growth of industrial democracy will produce better results than some juicy carrots for the economically successful donkey and a big stick to make sure of no non-sense from workers who hold up production while they argue about their rights? Once socialists enter into competition with their opponents on these grounds their case is, at best, inconclusive.

It is on quite different ground that socialists must take their stand. All the quantitative improvements which have so far been gained – less unemployment, higher wages, shorter working hours, increased pensions and more money for social services – are essential. But they are only the pre-liminaries to the real struggle for a qualitative change, for a society with a different content combining a fuller life for everyone with some finer, more co-operative way of living together. Here we are on the merest threshold of achieve-ment. Or have we been so poisoned by capitalist values that we have lost the taste for quality and cannot recognize how much there is that is still frustrating and degrading in the lives of our fellow men? Is the socialist vision now reduced to the familiar picture of a larger cake with bigger slices all round? If this were so, then capitalism, by conceding a little, would have won its greatest victory.

The socialist view of economic organization must remain

a qualitative one. It judges an economy by the quality of life it makes possible for every person. And in doing so it takes a man's life as a whole. It recognizes that people are affected by economic activities in two entirely different ways. On the one hand man is a consumer; he must eat to live, and as he advances in civilization he has other wants to satisfy besides. On the other hand, he is a producer; he only gets all he needs for life by working. When Adam was expelled from the Garden of Eden, so the Bible tells us, the Lord said to him : 'In the sweat of thy face thou shalt eat bread.' These words sum up the dual human results of any form of economic organization.

People's lives as consumers are influenced according to the range and type of goods and services that are open to them. Their lives as producers are influenced according to the kind of work they do and the way they are treated at their workplace. A human being is an indivisible entity; both aspects of his economic life are supremely important to him. In both of them the values of equality, freedom and fellowship have yet to be accepted.

3
EQUALITY OF OPPORTUNITY

The Meaning of Equality

'Socialism,' it has been said, 'is about equality.' From that no-one would dissent. Socialists have always agreed that in the society they want all men would be equal; this they have regarded as the very essence of their creed. Yet it is far from easy to see how men can be equal. In so many ways they are clearly not. They are unequal in their abilities – some are more gifted than others, some are stronger in body, mind or character. Their personal circumstances are unequal – some are single while others have large families to care for, some may be stricken by accident or ill-health. People are also unequal in their tastes and temperaments – some ask much more of life than others, some have wider interests or are more energetic and adventurous. Indeed, the more civilization progresses and the more that is known about man, the more apparent do his inherent inequalities become. What, then, is the meaning of equality as a socialist aim?

One recurring misunderstanding can be nailed down at once. Equality does not mean uniformity; to be equal is not to be the same. There is nothing egalitarian about a society which disregards individual differences and forces everyone into a uniform pattern of existence. For one thing, this would affect different people unequally. Independent and richly-gifted individuals would suffer more harshly from regimentation than those with placid natures who readily adapt themselves to their environment; a weak man would be more severely taxed by physical labour than a strong one. What is more, uniformity can never be achieved without a ruling class possessing rights entirely different from those who must submit to its rulings, for someone must design the strait-jacket and force others to wear it. The equality socialists demand is not concerned with the obliteration of variety. The very diversity of individual fulfilment is an enrichment of society, to be encouraged and cherished, not ironed out of existence.

It is not the differences which nature has ordained or fate decreed, against which socialists have protested; that would be nonsense. Their revolt has been against the privileges which society concedes to some and not to others. Why, they have asked, should some enjoy a favoured treatment simply because they happen to belong to a particular class or race or sex or social group? Every person, no matter what his origins or endowments, wants to make the most of his life in his own way. His claim to do so, without causing injury to others, deserves the same respect as the next man's. This is the sense in which all men are equal and Jack is as good as his master. It is an equality that rests, simply and surely, on their common humanity. Social privilege is the failure of society to accord this equal respect to the claims of all its members.

To-day most people, including many who do not call themselves socialists, would be prepared to accept this general conception of equality. They would not, in theory, deny anyone his right to make the most of his life. But to put the principle into practice involves social implications which are far less readily accepted. For what a man makes of his life depends on two things – his qualities and his opportunities. Society cannot determine his qualities, but it can determine his opportunities, and it is here that the principle of equality has its application. Whether a man can work, whether he can gain an adequate income with sufficient leisure in which to enjoy it, whether he has the possessions and amenities he requires, whether he has access to education and the common heritage of knowledge and culture, even whether he can inform himself correctly about what is happening around him, all this is largely outside his control. For these and many more of the opportunities which provide the basic substance of his life he depends on the organization of society. The more complex society becomes the greater the dependence, the fewer the exceptions who can push their own unaided way. If society is to treat all its members as equals, it must be organized to share out its opportunities without favour.

Does, then, the familiar slogan 'equality of opportunity' sum up all that we have in mind? That depends on what is meant by it. Sometimes it is taken to mean no more than that everyone should have an equal start in life; society should distribute no favours or handicaps at birth. This has been the liberal conception of equality, which comes closest to fulfilment in a society like that of the United States. It is part of what socialists want too, but only part. For however equal opportunities may be at the start of life, some people's qualities – and not necessarily their good ones – soon give them an advantage over others. The stronger may push the weaker to the wall, the ruthless may ride roughshod over the gentle; the unscrupulous may fill their pockets at the expense of the innocent. A society built on the ladder principle, which starts everyone off equally from scratch but allows some to reach the top by pushing others to the bottom, is clearly not a socialist society.

Equality of opportunity implies something more than an equal start with the race left to the swiftest. The one-legged man has to have his chance too. What socialists want is an equal chance for everyone, taking their lives as a whole. They are concerned with the whole bundle of opportunities which society distributes throughout a lifetime. But – and this is so often forgotten – because people have different capacities and needs, these opportunities cannot be the same for everyone. It is senseless to offer every child the same opportunity for a grammar school education, when what the backward child may require is a special school with teachers trained to deal with his particular difficulties. There is no point in offering the man who enjoys working with his hands the opportunity to become an administrator; what he wants is the opportunity to express his gifts for craftsmanship. It is not one ladder that is needed, but dozens – as well as a place in the sun for those with no aptitude for climbing ladders at all.

Equality of opportunity has two quite separate social implications. The first is that people with similar capacities should have similar opportunities, irrespective of differences in birth or circumstance. Access to the education they want, as well as to the jobs they aspire to, should be on merit and on merit alone. The second implication is that people of different capacities should be given opportunities which are different, but which are nevertheless equal in the total life-chance they offer for personal fulfilment.

So far, the first of these implications has dominated social-ist thought. It has been tied up with the protest against the division of society into classes. As a result of class divisions people with similar capacities do not have similar oppor-tunities; their opportunities depend on the class to which they happen to belong. All the members of one class, despite their varying capacities, have an entirely different range of opportunities from all the members of another class. Under capitalism the propertied classes have enjoyed opportunities superior in every respect to those of the propertyless classes – in education, in income, in leisure, in occupation, even in the care of their backward, ill, and aged. They have enjoyed these superior opportunities regardless of their personal qualities; it was sufficient to be born as one of them to par-ticipate in their privileges. The classless society, which has been the continuing inspiration of socialists, would give no one group these superior opportunities. They would be open equally to all who could use them. The elimination of class distinctions is thus a measure of the achievement of equality.

But it is not the full measure. There is also the second, and no less important aspect. Even if all class distinctions were wiped out, the inequalities inherent in man would remain. Society would still face the task of honouring the claim of every man to an equal chance in life. There would still be the weak and the strong, the bright and the backward, the lucky and the unlucky. These inequalities can never be eliminated but they can be prevented from becoming a source of social discrimination. Nature herself pays no regard to the ideal of equality, so that if the less fortunate are to have their fair share of opportunities, society must step in to redress the balance.

Equality among Consumers

What does equality mean in the life of man as consumer? The problem here turns on the share of goods and services which each person is entitled to consume. In the early days of capitalism, these shares grew increasingly unequal. The wealth enjoyed by a few grew apace, but the many were forced into a greater and greater dependence on the meagre wages of uncertain jobs. They could earn no more than was sufficient to keep themselves alive to go on working. Labour was treated like any other commodity. It was bought at the cheapest possible price, and not bought at all when there was no profit in the transaction.

But the workers regarded their labour as much more than a commodity. They revolted against the degradation to which their lives had been reduced and claimed their rights as human beings. They asserted that, in a country where so much wealth was being produced as in the Britain of the nineteenth century, every worker had at least the right to enough to enable him to live in some measure of comfort and dignity. They demanded 'a living wage'; and beyond that a 'national minimum', to hold no matter what the turns of fortune. Whether a man was old or ill or workless, he had still a right to this minimum so that he could live without constant anxiety for the morrow. The achievement of social security, which we have witnessed in our own generation, has been the culmination of this struggle for a bare minimum – always and for all.

But social security is only a first step towards social equality. Life is made more tolerable for the underdog, but an underdog he remains. Each may get his minimum, but how does it compare with the maximum? Equality means fair shares; and it is to fair shares that socialists, having achieved a measure of social security, increasingly turned their attention.

What are fair shares? Certainly not equal incomes. With some rare and queer exceptions, socialists have never believed in that. Income equality could only be enforced by a political tyranny at the cost of economic stagnation. In any case, it is a complete misreading of the socialist ideal. If people are to have an equal chance to make the most of their own lives, they must be able to vary their incomes as they wish, and to choose between more income or more leisure. There are times when a person wishes to work longer and harder to earn more; at other times he may prefer more leisure even if it means a modest income. Income equality also ignores the different nature of different jobs; it makes, for example, no provision to compensate those who have particularly unpleasant work to do.

Sometimes that elusive idea 'the just wage' has been pursued in an attempt to define fair shares. Justice obviously demands that people doing the same work should get the same wage; they should not get less because of their sex or race or any other chance distinction. Most people will also readily agree that it is only just to reward extra effort, whether it takes the form of greater physical or mental exertion, longer working hours or acquiring special skills. But how is it possible to measure these differences and fix a just wage to take account of all the differences in work? When we come to compare various occupations – coal-mining with school-teaching or baking bread with mending shoes – how decide whether one deserves a higher income than another, not to mention the riddle of fixing the exact amount? There is and can be no universal measuring rod to calculate all the niceties of what in justice is due to each.

The meaning of fair shares cannot possibly be expressed in exact monetary terms. It is not even important that it should be. As Professor R. H. Tawney has said:

What is repulsive is not that one man should earn more than others, for where community of environment, and a common education and habit of life, have bred a common tradition of respect and consideration, these details of the counting-house are forgotten and ignored. It is that some classes should be excluded from the heritage of civilization which others enjoy, and that the fact of human fellowship, which is ultimate and profound, should be obscured by economic contrasts, which are trivial and superficial.*

This is indeed the heart of the matter. What socialists wish to avoid are the extravagant differences of income which divide people into classes unable to mix on equal terms. The nearer we come to a society in which income is not a barrier to a common mode of life the nearer we approach fair shares. There is no other practical measure of its achievement.

But what of the inequalities which are not associated with class but arise out of the variations in individual circumstance? How are people to get their fair share of goods and services in times of sickness or old age, or when they are prevented from earning a living through any of the other vicissitudes of life? How are those who are physically or mentally or morally handicapped, maybe from birth, to be sure of any share at all? To meet these aspects of inequality is one of the functions of the social services.

The social services divide off into two broad categories. The first embraces the common services – such as education and health – of which every person has need at some time of his life. Originally these were working-class services; the rich required no social help. The principle on which they were based was to provide a minimum which people with a low income could not hope to procure for themselves. It was enough if the workers' children were given a few years of schooling and taught the three R's; or if the poor could have a bed in hospital in times of grave illness. To-day the aim is to free these services from their class distortions. Every child, regardless of the circumstances of his parents, should be covered by the same school system, and every person undergoing medical attention should have access to the same system of treatment. These services, it is now claimed, should be lifted right out of the sphere of

* R. H. Tawney, *Equality*, 1938 ed., p. 127

commercial considerations; they then become the cement of social unity.

The second category of social services are those with which we are more concerned here – the services which are designed to redress the individual inequalities due to circumstance or nature. These include the social incomes – family allowances, pensions, benefits – whose purpose is to tide over adverse circumstances, when the breadwinner cannot earn enough by work or is burdened by extra responsibility. They include, too, all the special services designed to redress hardships which nature imposes, by giving that special care and attention to the handicapped which the normal run of humanity do not require.

If people earned sufficient to make provision for all the contingencies of their lives – as many of the richer do to-day – then the community might be less called upon to maintain all these social services. Most people prefer to do what they can to look after themselves, within the limits of their means. The trouble is that those limits are soon exceeded when a person is faced with serious or prolonged adversity; then the community must help. There will always be those who get more than their fair share of adversity. Why should they get less than their fair share of opportunity as well? The individual who, through no fault of his own, is at a disadvantage compared with the generality of men, has a moral claim on the rest. And it is a claim not merely to be rescued from destitution, but to a range of opportunities roughly equal to those enjoyed by the community at large. The ideal of equality demands no less than that.

How far have we advanced towards equality for man as consumer? The preliminary stage of a national minimum is now within reach. Wages are, broadly speaking, enough to cover the necessities of life, and those who cannot work are sure of some sort of social income. The minimum social services have also been provided. Every child will have his years of education, every person will have medical treatment when he needs it, no one need go without some kind of roof over his head.

But all this is still only the minimum. The ultimate goal of fair shares still lies far ahead, at the end of a series of political battles yet to be won. That is not to say that no advance has been made at all. There has already been a very considerable levelling of incomes, which has blurred some of the old class divisions. Wage-earners and salary-earners, for example, can no longer be clearly separated into classes by their incomes, for some groups of manual workers are better paid even than some of the professional middle-classes. Within the ranks of the manual workers, differentials have been narrowed; the recent era of full employment has drastically altered the position of those who were once at the bottom of the scale.

Where, then, do we fall short? At both ends of the income scale there are still extremes – the extremely rich and the extremely poor. They are still set apart from the great mass of people who are tending gradually to a common mode of life. At the upper end there remains a class which is able to pursue an entirely different kind of existence. It is composed mainly of the top-salary earners with elastic expense accounts, and of the larger fortune holders in receipt of unearned income. This class can afford to live in large houses, to run expensive cars, to dine and entertain their friends in luxurious restaurants, where one meal may cost considerably more than the normal family's weekly food budget. It is irrelevant to point out that they may be only a tiny minority and that even if their incomes were spread over the rest of the population, it would only come to a few shillings a week more for each. Their scale of expenditure sets them apart from the community, and their ostentatious display continually mocks the ideal of equality.

At the other end of the income scale are those who depend on a social income to make ends meet. The plight of the old-age pensioners is notorious. Family allowances are still too small to enable the man with a large family to keep his end up unless he has a fairly large income as well. Even the national minimum attained after the war is threatened by the continual rise in prices. For all these people, just because they are dependent on the state, a bare minimum is thought to be enough. Society has not yet begun to look at their position in terms of fair shares.

It is in the social services in general that there is probably least appreciation of what equality implies. The common services are still by no means 'common' to all. The health service has gone a good way towards this ideal, but we still have an education system which, in spite of all improvements, continues to pay obeisance to the class divisions in our society. Those with more money are still more likely to have better educational opportunities than those with less. Even within the state system of education discrimination exists, the modern schools falling behind the grammar schools in esteem and often in numbers of staff and equipment. In the special services for the backward or disabled there is still a strong tendency to act as if the minimum were good enough. Mediocre facilities are thought to be sufficient for them. Mental hospitals are scandalously overcrowded and understaffed; services for the mentally deficient are woefully underfinanced; delinquents get only a fraction of the attention they need for rehabilitation. It is precisely for those who occupy the weakest position in our society that the ideal of equality is furthest from recognition.*

Equality among Producers

Equality among producers is concerned with the opportunities which people have in their work. Here, too, the industrial era began by giving the great majority of workers no rights at all. They were used or discarded as it suited the convenience of the employer. They were expected to work all hours, without holidays and under appalling conditions. They had to submit unquestioningly to the orders of their

* This is not to be taken as a general assessment of the social services; we are considering them here only from the economic point of view of how much money is spent on them.

'masters'. Whether they liked their work was a question few would have dreamed of asking.

The first stage of the struggle has been to establish minimum rights for all workers. Foremost among these was the right to a job. A job is not only a means of earning an income which, heaven knows, is important enough. It also represents honourable participation in the life of the community. No provision for doles can ever compensate for condemning a man to the degradation of enforced idleness, to the misery of eating out his heart because he is not wanted. It was not the dole that workers clamoured for, but 'the right to work'. This was the very minimum to which every man, as producer, felt he was entitled.

Attached to the job there are certain conditions to which workers have laid claim. A good wage, of course; but also protection from danger and, in so far as the trade permitted, a healthy and pleasant environment in which to work. Then the worker has called for a reasonable working-day and sufficient holidays. To-day he asks, further, for a measure of job security. If he loses a job at short notice, his whole life – and that of his family – may be upset, even though he can find alternative employment elsewhere. True, he can never be guaranteed absolute security in any particular job, because there will always be shifts in the economy. But that is no reason why he should be dismissed arbitrarily, regardless of his circumstances. All this adds up to social security for man as producer – the counterpart of social security in his life as consumer.

But this is not yet the equality which socialists demand. Conspicuous inequalities are still with us. Why should some people, with no greater inherent capacities than others, and only because they were born into the right families, have so much more opportunity to find a good job, and enjoy so much more satisfying and secure a working life? Why should some find every career open before them, while others have no alternative to manual work? And why – to take the questioning further – should not every man, whatever his capacities, find self-expression and contentment in work suited to him?

All these arbitrary inequalities in working life have as little justification as arbitrary inequalities in income. Much of a man's adult life is spent at work. If he is a misfit there; or if he is treated, day in and day out, with a thinly-veiled contempt, his whole life and the lives of those around him may be spoilt. Once he has grown out of childhood, the type of job he does and the esteem in which he is held as a worker, are decisive influences in his development. A higher standard of living or, for that matter, shorter working hours, cannot make up for a lifetime of frustration at work.

Not that equality for man as producer can possibly mean that everyone has the right to occupy any job he fancies; no form of economic organization can guarantee that. There can only be one Prime Minister at a time, even if several people would like to step into his shoes. What equality demands is that everyone shall have the chance to find not merely some kind of job, but a job that suits him.

Three conditions have to be observed to make of this right a reality. The first is that there should be no direction of labour. Direction always means that some are compelled to do work which others are unwilling to do; it is an absolute denial of equality, only to be justified in times of extreme emergency. The second condition is that everyone should have access to the training and education which allow him to follow his own particular bent, not only as an adolescent, but also in later life. The third condition is that there should be equality of access to jobs and to promotion on the basis of merit or seniority. There is no point in providing training when the way to advancement is barred by nepotism, or the snobbery of the old school tie.

But none of this settles one vital factor in working-life – the way a man is treated once he is at work. Most people earn their living to-day as employees of an organization. Their status within that organization is of the utmost importance to them. The socialist aim here is often expressed simply as 'equality of status', but what does that imply? In every work community there must be discipline; without a structure of authority there would be no organization at all. Some have to give the orders and others to carry them out. These differences cannot be levelled out, and there is no reason why they should be.

Equality of status must be looked at differently. What matters is not that everyone should wield the same authority but that every individual, regardless of organizational grading, should be treated as a person. He should enjoy certain amenities and conditions in common, his participation should be sought and his interests taken into account. Every member of the working community has something to offer, and his views – particularly as regards his own work – should be respected. If all contribute to the best of their abilities, no one should be made to feel that his opinions and preferences, even his convenience can be ignored – that what is not good enough for the other man must be good enough for him.

If equality for man as consumer is still out of reach, equality for man as producer is not even in sight. It is true that now, under full employment, most of the minimum rights have been established; and as long as full employment remains they are not likely to be violated. But the next phase, towards full equality in working-life, has scarcely started. Equal rights for producers have not even been formulated, let alone asserted.

This lack of equality still shows even in the simplest and most obvious things. Why should it be taken for granted that the conditions for a wage-earner must differ from those of the salaried staff? Why should a salaried man have more job-security, a better pension scheme, shorter hours of work, and longer holidays? Why indeed should workers be divided into 'wage-earners' and 'salary-earners', with all the snobbery implicit in the distinction? And why, in the actual arrangements at work, should one set of workers have better amenities – superior canteens and washrooms, for example – than others? Not that these distinctions apply only between wage and salary-earners. There is in fact a hierarchy of status between all grades in industry which is upheld by a whole variety of external arrangements.

Class distinctions among workers are seen, too, in the unequal opportunities in access to training and to jobs. This is not due only to differences in income. It is as much the result of our education system, with all the inequalities of opportunity which it embodies. It is the result, too, of the rigid ties between formal education and the occupation which his education entitles a man to follow. His life-long status is determined for him in his school days, and determined almost irrevocably. There are, in the words of Professor T. H. Marshall,

... no signs of any relaxation of the bonds that tie education to occupation. On the contrary, they appear to be growing stronger. ... A man of forty may be judged by his performance in an examination taken at the age of fifteen. The ticket obtained on leaving school or college is for a life journey.*

Thus it is rare in this country – unlike in some others – for a man who begins his working life as a wage-earner to have the chance of entering any of the higher salary-earning ranges of occupations. Quite apart from the professions, which obviously require a long and special education, the leading posts in industry largely remain a class monopoly. When the National Coal Board introduced its modest ladder scheme, which in fact did no more than extend the educational opportunities open to young miners, this was considered a dramatic innovation which other industries have not been in haste to imitate. Educational opportunities are, in any case, only one side of the problem. The crux of the matter is the facilities provided by industry for promotion.

All these persistent inequalities in the life of man as producer constitute one of the great challenges to socialists in our time. There is probably no place in this country where more unblushing class discrimination exists than in the

* T. H. Marshall, *Citizenship and Social Class*, 1950. p. 64.

workshop. Despite the changes brought about by full employment, the distinctions that remain stare one in the face. They are there in the terms of contract, in amenities, in opportunities for advancement, in all the subtle ways by which wage-earners are treated as a lesser breed. At their place of work, millions of men and women are daily subjected to treatment which would be considered intolerable in any other walk of life. The battle for equality here has not only to be won; it has yet to be joined.

4

TOWARDS FREEDOM

The Chance to Choose

Socialism is not only about equality; it is also, and even more fundamentally, about freedom. The only way of expressing the equality we seek is, as we have seen, in terms of freedom. The very phrase 'equality of opportunity' means fair shares of freedom; for every opportunity is a freedom, a chance to choose and to act according to one's choice. Just because freedom is the greatest possession of man, socialists have wanted it fairly distributed, not the precious monopoly of the few.

Even the worst of tyrants does not deny the value of freedom – for himself. What he denies is freedom for others. He extends his freedom to do what he chooses by stealing the freedom of his subjects. Every tyranny, indeed every form of exploitation, is a theft of freedom. Just as a robber stands with a gun and strips his victim of his property, so – though perhaps less conspicuously – a dictatorship or a class or a social group can use its power to enlarge its own freedom by stripping away the liberties of others. The struggle for equality is a struggle against the violation of other people's freedom.

Every man's freedom is relative; he can have more or less of it. One way of getting more for oneself is to filch it from others. But another way is to extend freedom's frontiers so that opportunities become more abundant for all. Man is constantly involved in a struggle with nature, including his own nature, to broaden the bounds of his freedom. Ignorance and lethargy can cause him to lose ground, knowledge and determination to gain it. This struggle for the enlargement of human freedom transcends the struggle for equality. Socialists are necessarily identified with it. For the same reason that they seek a fair distribution of freedom – so that each individual may have the opportunity to lead a full life – so they are also concerned that there should be more freedom or more opportunities to be distributed all round.

The struggle for more freedom knows no end. In the democracies we may speak about living in a free society as if an absolute liberty had been won and now needed only to be defended. This illusion springs from a narrow and negative conception of freedom as being identical only with an absence of political tyranny. But even in countries like our own, where certain basic political liberties are reasonably secure, the opportunities – the real positive freedoms – which they bestow on the individual are by no means a fixed quantity; nor is every individual's portion the same.

The same narrow and negative conception has been applied to economic freedom. Look at the familiar arguments used to defend capitalism in the name of freedom. Capitalism, it is said, gives man as consumer a free choice of goods and man as producer a free choice of jobs. He can walk into any shop and buy what he fancies; he can go into the labour market and seek the job he prefers. No law restrains him. If freedom means choice, what more can be asked?

But, workers have asked themselves, what is the use of the freedom to spend your money on what you please if your purse is empty? What solace is there in being able to move from one job to another when you are grateful to have any job at all? Or when you cannot acquire the education or resources to get the job you really want? No wonder that the capitalist defence of freedom has had so little appeal in the labour movement. Not that this freedom is worthless – on the contrary, it is prized by everyone – but in fact it was simply a rich man's privilege.

Economic freedom, like other freedoms, is much more than the absence of legal restraint; it is the sum of all the positive opportunities which people have in their economic lives. In primitive societies these opportunities are usually so scarce that economic freedom is minimal, even though no despot tyrannizes over his fellows. Man as consumer is bound to the serfdom of poverty, and man as producer to the serfdom of drudgery. Economic freedom broadens out as society advances. Consumers may then be able to throw off the shackles of poverty and know what it is to choose the goods and services they desire. Producers may liberate themselves from drudgery and find self-expression in the work that suits them best. The greater these opportunities, the wider are the bounds of their freedom.

Everyone, no matter what his political beliefs, must give lip-service to freedom; this is the supreme value for which man has always striven. It is not – and never has been – the denial of the value of freedom that stands in the way of its expansion. The obstacle lies rather in the partial and distorted views that obscure freedom's real meaning. Communists, for instance, justify their tyranny on the grounds that it means freedom from poverty. Capitalists have justified poverty in the midst of plenty for the sake of freedom from legal restraint. Many people are willing to condone a life of drudgery if it brings the freedom of a higher standard of living. None of these partial definitions of freedom pay man the respect of treating him as a whole. To be free he must be neither a pawn nor a pauper, nor a drudge; he must throw off all his chains.

Freedom through Plenty

The freedom of man as consumer depends on the range of goods and services available to him. The more plentiful these are, the easier his access to them, the greater his freedom. To enlarge freedom through plenty has been counted the great achievement of capitalism. Many primitive societies by contrast do not concern themselves with material plenty; custom, tradition, or simply lethargy turn thoughts in other directions. Life in these countries is therefore limited by poverty; man has no hope of acquiring many of the good things he needs to advance in civilization. In capitalist societies, on the other hand, the aim of high production has been strongly upheld, and with considerable success. It needs no reference to statistics to know that, under capitalism, production has increased so remarkably that the life of the great mass of consumers has been revolutionized within a century. Capitalism can be said to measure its success by the abundance of its output.

With this achievement before them, socialists have found it easy to believe that – at least in the capitalist countries – the problem of production was solved. For a time this certainly seemed to be no concern of theirs. Their task was rather to deal with the inequalities in the distribution of the stream of wealth pouring off the machines. But in recent years there has been a change in attitude. As the grosser inequalities in distribution are gradually levelled out, it becomes clear that if all are to have more, more will have to be produced. Added emphasis has been given by the needs of the underdeveloped lands. If they are to be helped too, there is no way but through an expansion of our – and their – output. Few socialists to-day would claim, as many were doing twenty years ago, that production is no problem. Few would question that without higher output freedom for the consumer cannot be much further extended; indeed in some countries, without higher output economic freedom can hardly be said to exist.

Do we come, then, to the popular cry of the post-war years 'Produce more! Produce more!'? Do capitalist and socialist values blend at this point into a common aim which stands above the political conflict, the only point of difference being which system will in fact produce more? Unfortunately this conclusion is being far too readily accepted within the labour movement. Quantity is becoming the only measure, the one criterion of success. There must always be more and more, regardless of what the 'more' comprises.

Quantity may understandably be the supreme test in a very poor nation; the most urgent need may be to have more of what already exists – more food, more clothes, more pots and pans, more houses of the simplest kind. When people have next to nothing, to feed and clothe and house them comes first. But as soon as the basic needs are met, the claims of quality become increasingly insistent. Mass production of cheap, perhaps shoddy, goods is not the summit of man's desire. Whatever we have to-day in the way of civilization has been created because quality was not always sacrificed to quantity. There have been some people rich enough to demand high quality products, to foster and value craftsmanship, to support the arts and sciences. A cultural tradition has been created, even if only a few were privileged to enjoy it.

But now we enter a new situation. The further we move towards equality of incomes, the less can private fortunes maintain this tradition. If there is to be a concern for what is meant by 'quality', society must provide it; society must care for all those consumers' needs which cannot be bought by the private purse or created out of private demand alone. How else are there to be parks and sports grounds, libraries and concert halls, universities and institutes, town planning and community centres? How else are people to gain access to knowledge, beauty, and culture?

Not everyone may care for these things. If some prefer to spend their leisure in gambling, no one has the right to force them to listen to music. But, equally, those who want music should not be denied it. The market can be relied upon to provide the dog tracks and football pools, but not the orchestras, for there is not enough money to be made out of them. The market will build houses of a sort, but it will not lay out towns that are a pleasure to live in, for that is not always a commercial proposition. The market will see to it that goods in demand are produced, but it will not set new standards, it will not cater for minority tastes, and it will not guarantee that what is produced is of a quality to take pride in.

There will always be controversy as to where the balance should be struck between personal and social spending. It is easy to win a cheap popularity by promising to cut down public expenditure and so reduce taxation, for most people assume all too readily that it is 'better' that they should have more to spend themselves even if it means less is spent on the enduring things that enrich the whole community. It falls, surely, to socialists to insist on a broader conception of consumers' freedom than the fatness of the private purse. How can one argue that the individual's choice to spend as he wants is the greatest good, in the face of the ugly and dreary heritage which capitalism has left us? Look at our slatternly cities, at our despoiled countryside, at the level of our education, at the mediocrity of our tastes and standards. Wherever this generation has seen an improvement, it is because of increasing social expenditure in one form or another. At every turn the difference this has already made to human enjoyment and the enrichment of our cultural life is evident, whether it be in preserving the open spaces, in subsidizing the ballet, in the great work of the B.B.C. or in such simple pleasures as listening to the band in the park. To all this growth of consumer's freedom, the play of the market has contributed next to nothing.

In contrast to this achievement of more recent years, consumer's freedom is being increasingly menaced by the strong pressures of private interests. Daily, immense resources are being employed to persuade people that certain things are the most desirable to acquire; indeed that the possession of more and more of certain material things is the be-all and end-all of living. More money is now being spent in this country on advertising than on education. Who can say that it is a free and conscious decision of consumers that they want this amount of the nation's wealth diverted to advertisements which only add to prices and often confuse the purchaser's intelligent choice? Much of the advertising is designed for no other purpose than to push competitive products. No one is enriched by the high-powered salesmanship which foists half a dozen different detergents, doing much the same job, on to the market, or persuades people into drinking more of one make of beer rather than of another. It may be better that customers are induced by advertisement and propaganda to buy certain things, rather than forced by the government, but both are forms of mass manipulation – the difference is only one of degree.

Even apart from the distorting influence of the advertiser, the consumer often has no sure guide to quality. Prices give him none, and he has no other way of knowing which of a line of products is well made and trustworthy. Some may be positively injurious, but no one tells him so. The market will not, because it is geared only to the purpose of making money by whatever means the law permits, and every prospective consumer is fair game. If he is not actually a dupe, he is likely to be an innocent abroad. To advise and protect him is a duty which must be undertaken by society. Freedom of consumer's choice, like all freedoms, must be guarded and it must be informed.

Freedom in Work

If freedom for consumers has been too narrowly understood, freedom for producers has scarcely been understood at all. Capitalism held that it was freedom enough if everyone could be said to have a free choice among the jobs available to him. Mostly this free choice was a myth. Far from picking and choosing, workers considered themselves lucky to have any job, however distasteful. Even where jobs were offered, few workers had the training to aspire to those which really attracted them. Socialists have therefore gone further and insisted that choice would only really be free when it was not fettered by fear of unemployment or by lack of educational opportunity. But few have moved on to ask how much freedom a man experiences in his job once he has it, whether it crushes or cultivates his individuality. This aspect of freedom is seldom considered to be of concern to society; indeed the effect of his work on the worker is rarely given a moment's thought.

What does freedom in work mean? It means the chance to do work in which the individual can find self-expression. If a job demands skill, discretion, responsibility, if in some way it commands interest, then it provides an outlet for self-expression. We all know this to be true. A surgeon holding the lives of people in his hands, exercising judgement and

44

skill of a high order, continually expresses his personality in his work. The same may be true of a teacher responsible for a group of children whose interests he can develop and whose characters he can help to form. If he is a good teacher he finds a sense of freedom and an abiding joy in his task. Whatever their walk of life people on the whole like to feel that things depend on them, that the particular contribution they are able to make counts for something in the common pool. Even those who are inclined to avoid responsibility enjoy exercising a skill, be it of the humblest kind; it is then that they express themselves most fully.

Even when the job itself provides small chance of self-expression, opportunity may come through working within a community, feeling that one counts there and that one's contribution is valued. To be esteemed by one's fellows and to participate in good working relationships is an enlargement of any man's personality. Status, esteem, good fellowship are often as important to a worker as wages and material conditions; they combine to give him a sense of freedom and significance.

But the great technological progress which has changed the face of industry in these last generations takes no account of such considerations. Industry has grown in scale regardless of the human or the social cost. Masses of people are brought together daily, irrespective of the time and effort they waste in travelling or, for that matter, what it costs the community. They are herded into work places in such numbers that each feels lost and insignificant among the hundreds or even thousands of other workers.

Within such massive organisms, work has itself been so divided and subdivided, so broken down into its smallest components, dependent on exact timing down to a fraction of a minute, that each man can only see himself as a small cog caught up in the inexorable revolutions of a giant wheel. He is allowed as much personality as the machine he tends – sometimes even less. And this fragmentation of work demands in turn a complicated hierarchy of supervision and management to ensure that each man's effort fits exactly into the mechanism, so that the wheel is kept turning continually. At the bottom of the hierarchy is the ordinary worker, who must be marshalled and organized, his responsibility taken from him; he is dependent for all he does on strict orders from some remote authority. Each individual is swallowed up in an intricate system, virtually impossible for him to understand. It becomes too great an effort of the imagination to relate what he is doing to the whole work process. In every significant respect he is cramped, cabined, and confined. Not all work is of this nature; there are plenty of jobs which call for a high degree of personal discretion, even outside the professions. But the general and accepted trend has been towards a mounting loss of freedom in work, which reaches its supreme expression in the bondage of the assembly-line.

We have only to look around at the greater part of manual, or for that matter non-manual, work in industry to-day to see the consequences. Its most obvious feature is an unrelenting monotony. It consists to a large and ever-increasing extent of dull, repetitive tasks which contribute nothing but boredom to the life of the worker. He has no say in how he does a job and does not know why he is doing it. What can his work mean to him, then, but a necessary evil to be endured for the sake of the pay-packet that comes at the end of the week? The only interest it can provide is the interest of earning money. Some consolation can perhaps be found in earning more or in the personal friendships formed at the place of work. But no one expects the work itself to give the worker any pleasure, let alone enrich his personality.

All kinds of excuses are advanced to defend this state of affairs in industry. It is said, for example, that most workers are happy if they have a nice easy job which makes no demands on them as long as it pays good money. They prefer a safe routine because it allows them to gossip and daydream. They dislike the responsibility which comes with greater freedom. Are these convenient assumptions really true? There is evidence enough to contradict them. Anyone familiar with the inside of a workshop knows how often workers go out of their way to create some interest in their work and to seize any chance to escape from a set routine. Previously apathetic men and women reveal quite unexpected capacities and enthusiasms when given the opportunity to express something of their own personality.

The contention that people are 'happy' as they are, has been a steady favourite with the opponents of social reform. Once it was said that the workers were 'happy' without education, so why educate them? Then it was said that they were 'happy' living in slums; they would only ruin new houses and keep their coals in the bathtub. Now it is said they are 'happy' engaged in a monotonous job, they like being told exactly what to do. Give them more freedom in their work and they will find it a burden.

There may be some truth in this argument. Not everyone is anxious to take on responsibility; not everyone objects to repetitive work. But there are many who do, and they have no alternative but to accept their lot. Many more still might be made aware of new satisfactions which work could offer them, if only they had the experience of something different. For people's attitudes are conditioned by what they know, and what they have been brought up to expect. Even happiness may be found by coming to terms with what appears to a man to be his inescapable fate.

Another popular excuse is that people can make up in their leisure hours for what they miss at work. There are many workers, it is said, who do not object to even the dullest work if only they have sufficient free hours. That might be the case if working hours were short enough. But it remains a fact that people have to work the greater part of the day, and that their work is bound to take up an even greater part of their energies. Why should all that time and effort go into a stultifying activity? Why should they be deprived of the important experience which creative work can, and should, be in everyone's life? There is this, too, to be considered. If men are conditioned to a passive role in their work, they are likely to be passive in their leisure as well. In our modern civilization people have increasingly become onlookers in their recreations and entertainment, instead of participants as they used to be in the days when ready-made enjoyments were not so easily available. Freedom is indivisible; destroy it and the taste for it in one place, and it is easily destroyed elsewhere.

Then comes the final, the thought-to-be-conclusive argument, that if we want efficiency and high productivity, we cannot afford the luxury of freedom at work. But why is that conclusive? Why have we to assume that the best way of increasing output is to turn the worker into a robot? This may be the prevailing assumption among technicians, but it is by no means proven. The subdivision of labour has advantages for efficiency, but it has its disadvantages too. It may so rob the worker of all interest in his work, that he sinks into apathy, exerts himself no more than he need, opposes change and resists every improvement. Human beings are not machines; they may work best just when they are free and their capacities are given rein. Who knows where the balance of advantage really lies?

But wherever this balance lies, one thing is clear. The craftsman's day, when men knew the freedom of independent work, is over, for the great run of industry. The machine is now with us and it cannot be dismantled. Even if it were possible to set the clock back on an historical process, no one really wants to do that. For the machine is paradoxical in its effects. On the one hand it releases man from physical drudgery and makes the fruits of his work abundant. On the other it introduces the subdivision of labour and binds him to a set routine in a highly complex organization. The problem is to retain the advantages of technological progress and at the same time to minimize its social cost.

There is no reason to despair of a solution to this problem once it is seen as a problem and squarely faced. It can be solved, just as other problems are, once there is a will to do so. Even though it would be folly to turn back on the use of machines, the organization of work around the machine can be altered; so can the way machines are designed to fit into the work organization. It has often been pointed out, for instance, that the increasing use of electrical power makes it less and less necessary for industrial processes to be concentrated under one mammoth roof. Parts of the process can just as well be decentralized; it is certainly no more expensive in terms of social costs to move the finished components once a month to a central point for assembly than it is to move men backwards and forwards every day.

Technical development does not take place blindly, but in accordance with social demand. Its effects become harmful when society demands nothing but increased output and ignores the consequences to the worker. This is what has been happening. In order to make the machine the servant of man as consumer, it has been permitted to stride into mastery over man as producer. But this need not be so. If society demanded a care for the producer, the machine and the organization that goes with it could be made his servant as well. The recent developments in automation may well provide the great opportunity for this revolutionary change of emphasis.

Just as there can now be no turning back on the machine, so there can be no turning back on large-scale organization, however far one may go with decentralization. But like the machine, the large organization is a paradox. On the one hand it may reduce each individual worker to insignificance; but, on the other, it opens new opportunities before him. What he loses in his individuality and personal discretion, he may gain in a new consciousness of a community effort and a new world of work relationships. He is no longer an isolated workman, perhaps cut off during the long working hours from all social contact, but a member of a group offering him new chances of self-expression. In the same way as machine processes can be shaped – if the will is there – to suit the needs of the workers, so can industrial relations be moulded so as to draw forth their willing participation. It depends on what society calls for.

Yet in the end a choice may sometimes have to be made between higher output and more freedom in work. There may be a price to pay for this freedom. The point is that the choice is a valid one, the price may be worth paying. Higher output meets one kind of human need; freedom in work meets another. Why should it always be taken for granted that the first is to be preferred to the second? If the two conflict, why should the latter not sometimes be preferred? To ask for freedom in work may perhaps be the assertion of a better sense of values than any embodied in the statistics of production.

5

TOWARDS FELLOWSHIP

The Fabric of Society

When socialists started on their struggle, one consideration dominated their thoughts. The rights of the workers were disregarded under the harsh economic system in being; in the name of equality and freedom they had to be asserted and established. A century of concentrated effort has certainly brought its victories, yet the rights of workers are still incomplete. Men are not yet equals in industry – far from it; and there is still only a glimmering of understanding of all that freedom here might imply. But at least this has been gained – the workers now have more than their chains to lose; they have a stake in society, something to defend and extend. They have, too, the means to fight further through the organizations which have won them their present achievements. The struggle will continue – but is that all that is needed? Will it suffice to go on in the ways that served us well in the past?

It will not. A point is now coming when the assertion of rights will yield little more, even when it is backed by power. No society, socialist or otherwise, can live by rights alone. Its very fabric disintegrates if everyone thinks only of what is his due, chases his own satisfactions, stubbornly insists on his pound of flesh. Each right has its corresponding obligation which someone must honour. Who is that someone to be?

As long as the workers were deprived of everything except their crudest subsistence, socialism was a philosophy of claims rather than of obligations; there was nothing that labour could give more than it was already giving. The workers claimed a larger share of the product of their labour; the poor claimed education for their children; the sick claimed medical attention; and the old claimed pensions to see them through their years of retirement. It was the task of the state to meet these claims, and the job of socialists to see that it did so. The obligations to pay and to help rested on the privileged classes alone. So unequal were the blessings that society had bestowed, that in justice the poor had to demand and the rich to give.

As the balance within society is redressed, obligations become more equally spread. The rich are no longer so disproportionately rich that they can pay for everything, nor the poor so disproportionately poor that they can pay for nothing. Anyway, there is so much more to-day that must be paid for. Now that we have social services for everyone, there is an obligation upon everyone to contribute something to their cost. Now that wages have risen above the subsistence level and everyone is employed, wage-earners have also to pay their share of income tax. People who want a higher standard of living have to work harder to get it; they cannot merely take it from someone else. Socialism can no longer make new conquests simply by demanding rights; it must also ask from everyone his share of obligations. What each person now considers his due cannot possibly be provided unless the whole community, every section of it, accepts its responsibilities.

What induces people to accept responsibilities? Some duties can be legally enforced – to pay taxes, to respect a contract of employment, to give full measure to a customer. These legal obligations can never be more than the barest minimum. All the attitudes – the consideration, the care for the other man's interests, the fair dealing in everyday things – which are needed if every man is to have his due, cannot possibly be legislated for and secured by a police force. They depend, and must always depend, on each person's voluntary behaviour. If people are to live together with some degree of comfort and pleasure, let alone in conditions of equality and freedom, there must be a willing recognition of all sorts of obligations, down to such simple things as not despoiling the countryside with litter or keeping your neighbour awake with a radio at full blast.

Obligations are accepted when people feel identified

with the community, not rebels against it; when they care about its welfare and know that their contribution counts. This community feeling cannot be achieved only by changing the state; society must be changed as well. Society is a network of loyalties which bind people to each other and make each feel responsible for something more than his own advantage. These are the loyalties which have to be strengthened, if the fabric of a socialist society is to be woven.

Indeed, what is required is something more than an acceptance, perhaps a grudging acceptance, of obligations. There is a still more far-reaching ideal of social relations which socialists have always cherished – the ideal of fellowship. Fellowship is not only giving every man his due; it means going out of one's way to help him. It starts with the courtesy and neighbourliness which can be infused into everyday life, and broadens out into the higher reaches of selfless community service. It is a sense of kinship extending far beyond the limits of the family.

The well-known words of William Morris, 'Fellowship is life, lack of fellowship is death' express a theme which has been repeated again and again in the annals of socialist thought. Capitalism has been condemned, not only for its injustices, but because it split society into classes and pitted men against their neighbours; it drove its victims into rebellion so that they recognized no loyalty except to their fellow-victims. Socialism, in contrast, was born of the conviction that a society could be created in which man, no longer forced into a competitive struggle for survival, no longer a prey to injustice, would rejoice in the opportunity of serving his community. This has always been the socialist belief, but sometimes in the daily struggle for more and more, here and now, it has been forgotten. It is time to remind ourselves of it afresh.

Unrecognized Responsibilities

To-day most socialists would agree that the day is past when workers could talk only of their rights; they know that obligations must be accepted as well. All the pressures for higher productivity, all the propaganda that a rising standard of living depends on increased production, have hammered home the point. Nor does anyone challenge fellowship as a fine ideal. But what do these conceptions really mean? What exactly is asked of people in their economic life?

The law itself imposes certain demands. Of the consumer it asks that he should pay his taxes and so give up to the community part of the income that he might otherwise have enjoyed in his own way. What is asked legally of man as producer is embodied in the contract of employment. Certain duties are put on employers and employees alike – so many hours of work for so many pounds in wages, so many days in holidays, such and such conditions for safety and health. The law safeguards against gross injustice and calls for a minimum contribution from everyone, but it can do no more.

Anything beyond this must be given voluntarily. No one can force the consumer not to waste the goods or abuse the services which the community provides. He must see for himself that it is wrong to do so, because he would be robbing, not the government or the rich (which would anyhow be a poor justification) but his own neighbours. If the nation's resources are squandered, the general standard of living must sooner or later suffer. If the social services are abused, their further development is hindered. Everyone who flouts this simple morality is an exploiter, even if he does not wear a top hat and smoke a cigar.

But the main voluntary obligations fall on man as producer, and the first of these is the obvious one of doing a good job of work. The effect of one man's work on the welfare of the whole of society may seem negligible; it is hard for him to believe that it matters very much whether he puts his heart into it or not. Yet work is a primary means of participation in society at large, the direct and practical way in which each makes his contribution to the whole. If no social responsibility is recognized here, it is unlikely

54

to be recognized in the higher reaches of community service.

Work not only gives a man his self-respect; it provides him with the opportunity to respect the interests of others. One sees this clearly enough in a service occupation, when the worker comes face to face with the consumer and bad work immediately causes inconvenience and strained relationships. It is no less true in a factory where a shoddy performance must eventually cause some purchaser to suffer. Nothing, short of a pistol at their heads, can compel people to accept this straightforward obligation of citizenship, if they do not wish to. Yet it is surely clear beyond argument that, unless they do, the economy is like a house built on sand.

A different range of obligations arises out of the fact that people nowadays work together in considerable numbers; as a rule they are employed in fairly large organizations with a complex structure of relationships. These, too, cannot be regulated by law. But if industry is to do its job the relationships must be good; each employee of the organization has to have a care for the interests of those with whom he works. What matters is not only how everyone does his own job, but how he behaves to the others in the doing of it – how managers treat workers, or workers treat managers, or workers treat their fellow-workers.

This is where the ideal of fellowship must find expression in economic life, if it is to find any expression at all. In practical terms this means that everyone employed in a business enterprise must be an active participant in its conduct, carrying a feeling of responsibility for its success, and striving to make it a model of good relations and fair treatment. Not every man wants to sit on committees, but if he feels responsible he will show his interest in what is done at the committee level and will be concerned about all the daily happenings on the shop floor. He will play his part in creating a sense of community and good comradeship.

Why does so little of this spirit exist in industry to-day? The great majority of those employed in it, whether as managers or as workers, seem to recognize no obligations apart from those enforced by agreements and laws. They do what they have to and wash their hands of further responsibility. It surely calls for comment that men who are good citizens in their leisure hours, devoted fathers and kind neighbours, suddenly ignore the most elementary claims of citizenship as soon as they enter the workshop.

That people behave in this way in industry is not just an unhappy chance. We are reaping now the harvest of earlier sowings. The worker's attitude to-day is the result of past failures to recognize his rights. He can hardly be expected to accept obligations with a good grace when others have not honoured their obligations towards him. An employer's appeal to a worker to be 'loyal' to his firm is bound to be resented as long as the firm shows precious little loyalty to him. It is pointless to ask people to act responsibly while they are being denied responsibility and considered unfit even to be consulted. It is equally pointless to ask them to take an interest in their work when nothing is done to make work interesting. So long has the worker been badly treated, so little has his dignity been respected, so deeply have class-divisions rent society, that now that full employment and strong organization have given him a greater sense of power, he is naturally inclined to assert his own wishes. Service still seems to him a continuation of servitude. Any attempt to drum home his obligations is likely to be treated as yet another Sunday school lesson, or resented as a weakening of the militancy which it has been the socialist aim to arouse.

What, then, should be done? Have we to wait until the last vestiges of class privilege are wiped out before workers will become responsible participants in their work and take the ideal of fellowship seriously? This would be to put one's faith in miracles. No one seriously believes that, under our democratic methods, a day will suddenly come which everyone will recognize as the opening of a new era, and all those who have previously sought their own undisguised advantage, will immediately be transformed into servers of their fellow-men. Something must be done now to change the texture of economic life, to introduce the new forms and values which will in time make fellowship a realizable ideal.

The Purposes of Industry

The only way to eliminate this bitter legacy of the past is to get to the bottom of the problem. That lies in the very purposes to which the whole of our economic activity is geared. To change these purposes should now be the object of all the militancy that can be commanded. For the twentieth century has inherited the obnoxious doctrine that the only purpose of work in industry is to make money. This is the great curse handed down to us from the industrial revolution, a curse from which we have never freed ourselves. As the Hammonds wrote:

The town of the industrial age ... expressed a concentration in which religion, beauty, leisure, the life of the spirit, or the life of the senses, were all held to be rivals to the stern life of selfish duty. The purpose of man's life was not to fight or to pray, to contemplate or to create, to enjoy or to become, but to make profits, profits for himself, if a master, profits for another, if a servant. This was man's duty, and it was the duty of society to put no obstacles in the way.*

According to this grim heritage, people worked to grow rich, and industry gave everyone his opportunity. Work was not seen for what it really is – a basic social function through which man makes his contribution to society and gains his status in it. It was not understood as a prime means of personal fulfilment ranging from an outlet for sheer physical energy to the satisfaction which comes from achievement or from working in a team. Man is above all a social being. Each worker has to feel that he is furthering the ends of society; in doing so he is accepting a responsibility without which the human character cannot develop. None of this

* J. L. and B. Hammond, *The Rise of Modern Industry*, 1944 ed., p. 222.

was recognized; making money was all that mattered and wealth alone the gauge of success or failure. Colossal prizes could be won by the lucky entrants in the money race, and everybody else had to run all the faster towards the same winning post, if they were not to fall by the wayside.

Many things have changed, but to this day the old capitalist values have lost little of their vigour. The degrading conception of work still exists. True, we no longer tolerate the same mad scramble for money, in which the devil not infrequently took both the foremost and the hindmost. The drive for equality of opportunity has evened out some of the handicaps at the start of the race, and there is now a social ambulance to pick up the casualties. But the race goes on, even if more slowly.

To-day the lust for money is often concealed behind the more attractive demand for higher output. Productivity has now become the golden idol from whom all blessings flow, and to whom no sacrifice must be denied. But this is no more than a change of name. The appeal to personal gain is less conspicuous and probably less potent, but the effect on those caught up in the industrial system is much the same. What is still held as an ideal for behaviour in industry would never be tolerated elsewhere – whether in politics, or the professions or the arts. Why, then, should we be surprised if workers, when they cannot be tempted or driven, are indifferent and irresponsible? Having secured their pay-packet, why worry further? That is all they are supposed to be working for.

This indifference has been accentuated by the growth in scale of modern enterprise and the results are before our eyes. Workers feel less able to influence things at their place of work; they find it increasingly difficult to identify themselves with any purpose there, even to grasp the consequences of their own actions. There is then bred that fatal distinction between 'them' and 'us'; the resentment against feeling insignificant; the corroding cynicism of the 'couldn't care less'. There are large sections of the economy to-day where it can be said that the unaided effort of relating one's activities to those of one's fellows has become too great. Unless something is done to counteract these consequences, men inevitably relapse into a mere collection of individuals, valuing their work to the extent that it yields sufficient income. Beyond that they see it only as a purposeless activity, to be pursued at the behest of a remote authority who, to preserve one's self-respect, must be outwitted whenever the chance comes.

The very purposes of industry have to be changed if these attitudes are to be reversed. Industry has been allowed to develop as if it were an impersonal mechanism standing right outside society. It was there to turn out an ever-increasing flow of products and incomes. What it otherwise did to men was of no account. No one was in business for his health – still less for the health of others. To-day the government is expected to keep an eye on the efficiency of the industrial mechanism and to correct some of its more unfortunate results. Economists, using their measuring rod of money, are available as competent engineers. There are even industrial consultants and experts in 'human relations' to assist in reducing friction. But the myth that the purposes of industry are beyond the control of society remains unchallenged. There is nothing for it but to accept, passively, the growing human sacrifice which economic progress appears to demand.

This surely is the crux of our present economic dilemmas. In the past the wheels of industry turned well regardless of the attitudes of the workers it employed. Fear of poverty and unemployment made every factory a prison, and prisons can be run without paying more attention to the feelings of prisoners than the minimum needed to stave off revolt. Society and industry both accepted these same inhuman values and reinforced each other. But society has now begun to move away from industry and to destroy the compulsions on which industry relied.

This has had two consequences. Industry has become more dependent on the voluntary loyalty of its workers, and nobody willingly gives his devotion to any venture with which he does not feel identified. At the same time the worker's resentment grows as he experiences the contrast between his rights as a citizen in a democratic society and his role in the workshop where he is treated as little more than a digit in an economic calculus. In short, a century of socialist agitation, which has changed so much in society at large, has made little impact on the values which permeate industry. This divorce between industry and society cannot be maintained for long; it is at best a position of unstable equilibrium. Either society must go backwards – and this a powerful labour movement will resist to the full – or industry must go forwards.

PART TWO

The Choice of Means

6

LEARNING FROM EXPERIENCE

The ends of a socialist economy are to be found in the ideals of equality, freedom, and fellowship. By what means are these ends to be realized? Socialists have always recognized that something more than a change of heart was needed if their values were ever to become the common currency of economic life. The way the economy was organized had to be changed as well. But there agreement has ended. Innumerable programmes for immediate action have been proposed, and all kinds of blueprints for a socialist economic system have been prepared. Indeed, controversy among socialists on the measures to bring about socialism has been just as vigorous as the controversy for and against socialism itself.

It could hardly have been otherwise. No one can foresee exactly what the results of any proposed change in economic organization will be, and socialists, like everyone else, are likely to vary in their judgements. In the last resort the only sure guide in the choice of means is experience. But less than half a century ago socialism existed only in the realms of propaganda and prophecy; there was no experience to go on. Every socialist could then design his own Utopia untroubled by the painful necessity of facing any facts other than the dismal reality around him and his own determination to change it.

Those days are now at an end. With power has come the possibility of action. Measures which once were only argued about have been put into practice, and experience as to their working has gradually accumulated. It has, understandably, brought some unexpected lessons. Radical transfers of ownership have not realized all the hopes that were pinned on them, whereas great reforms have come about by means which had never figured prominently in socialist thought.

When a movement reaches this point in history – the point of reassessment – only a readiness to reconsider its means will save it from decline. This, surely, is how every virile cause advances – through continual reassessment in the choice of its means. There will always be those who refuse to learn from experience; who cling to what they imagine to be the dogmas of the established church and condemn any attempt to revise them as heresy. These are the architects of disaster. For facts are telling arguments, which cannot for long be ignored without disillusionment.

Take a parallel from the medical profession. Its ends – to prevent and to cure disease – do not change, but over the years its methods have altered. As knowledge advances, old remedies are continually being discarded and new ones take their place. No one would dream of blaming the doctors for changing their ideas; on the contrary, they would be re-garded as quacks if they clung to some earlier panacea which had failed to prove its worth. The same is true in politics. What is now asked of socialists is to adhere un-flinchingly to their ends, but to choose their means afresh; and to choose them in the light of the knowledge which was denied to their predecessors.

7
ECONOMIC SECURITY

The Struggle for Security

We start with the experience of a whole century of struggle on the part of a growing labour movement. Its main outcome can be stated quite simply. A measure of economic security has been brought into the life of every member of our society. This is the great achievement embodied in the Welfare State.

It is easy to understand why economic security was given first priority among the aims of organized labour; it is the essential foundation of all else. The quest for security has nothing to do with choosing a safe and comfortable life in preference to one filled with excitement and adventure; this choice is open only to those who are already sure of their daily bread. Whatever way of life different people may prefer, they all need enough to live on without being dependent on the charity of others or tormented by the constant fear of destitution. The most basic of all economic freedoms is freedom from the fear of want.

Yet doubt about their daily bread was the usual lot of the majority of working people. The propertied and educated classes had no fear of want; their privileges allowed them to take their security for granted. The rest had to compete with each other for the chance to work for an employer. As there were more workers than jobs available, competition kept their wages at a bare subsistence and left them at the employer's mercy. Even when employed, the workers lived in constant fear of unemployment, and of a future when they would no longer be worth employing.

The workers had no economic security because they had no protection; the state protected only the rights of property and the preserves of the professions. Originally they could not even protect themselves for they were denied the right of combination. What more natural, then, than that security should be their first, deeply desired, goal? They wanted security against adversity and, beyond that, security in work. It was these early struggles to gain some protection against the hazards and hardships of a chaotic existence that brought the labour movement into being.

The struggle for security has passed through three phases. The progress achieved during the nineteenth century – the first phase – was mainly the result of voluntary organization. The minimum of protective legislation that existed in the Factory Acts merely prevented workers being employed under inhuman conditions. Much more significant were the efforts of the workers themselves. They formed friendly societies to practise mutual aid. They sought to free themselves from dependence on capitalist enterprise by establishing their own co-operative trading. The skilled craftsmen were among the first to band together in trade unions so as to control, by their own working rules, the supply of their labour and its terms of employment. Increasingly other workers, as well, fought for and secured their right to bargain collectively, and found in their unions the means to regulate and protect the conditions of their working lives. Not least, in the solidarity of their own ranks they gained the deeper security of belonging to a society where they counted and were wanted, not as hands but as human beings.

Yet voluntary organization in all its forms could at best only provide a limited security for a limited section of the workers. The great appeal of socialism, perhaps the most important reason why it won the workers' support, was its promise of a universal solution to the problem of insecurity. With the growth of the Labour Party in the present century, the struggle entered a second phase. The rising political power of Labour lifted this problem out of the limited range of voluntary effort and compelled the government itself, through legislation, to accept some responsibility for establishing minimum standards for all. It became the accepted duty of governments to have a care for the subsistence of every citizen, and to tax the rich so that the poor might be supported. The first social service legislation was introduced. In industry this was paralleled by the winning of full acceptance for the principle of collective bargaining, with its implication that wages and working conditions should be regulated by agreements and not left to the free play of the market. When workers were too weakly organized to insist on their own rights, the government was called upon to provide statutory bodies to do the job. One aspect of *laissez faire* had now been abandoned; legislation and government action were accepted as the means for providing against adversity and supporting the regulation of the terms of employment.

But workers had still not achieved security. The legislation which had been introduced still gave them only a partial protection, and unemployment, their most insidious enemy, remained unconquered. Indeed, the aftermath of the first world war, with its mounting unemployment, had raised the problem of insecurity to new dimensions, which were further exaggerated by the great depression of 1929. The Labour government in office at that time seemed powerless to check the growing numbers of unemployed. Disillusionment with democratic socialism set in – in this and other countries. Neither trade union action nor social legislation could offer a cure for the recurring and deepening economic crises, which threatened even the gains already won.

Nor was it only the life of the workers which was rendered insecure by economic fluctuations. Every section of the community was touched to some extent. Insecurity became something more than the simple threat of destitution. In one way or another it affected the whole population, the stability of all their incomes; indeed it had begun to threaten, and in some countries destroyed, democratic institutions themselves. Unless the fluctuations in the economy were controlled, there could be no security for anyone or anything.

These were the circumstances in which a new demand arose – the demand for economic planning, and with it the struggle for security entered its third phase. The Keynesian revolution in economic thought had destroyed the myths of financial orthodoxy which had previously blocked the way to economic planning and helped to paralyse even the best-intentioned Labour governments. The second world war gave the practical impetus to develop the machinery for democratic planning, and demonstrated its potentialities. The return of a strong Labour government in 1945 supplied the political will to maintain and extend this machinery for peacetime needs. Full employment was now, at last, a reality, and on this firm ground it became possible to complete the edifice of the Welfare State. For the first time a comprehensive system of social insurance covering the whole population from the cradle to the grave was introduced, and most of the gaps in the system of voluntary and statutory regulation of wages and working conditions were filled.

Planning has now come to stay. Whatever theoretical arguments may be adduced against it, there is no turning back on what experience has proved. It is no longer a matter of practical debate whether to plan or not to plan; the only open questions are what to plan and how to plan it.

Full Employment without Inflation

Planning for economic security means, first and foremost, planning to maintain full employment.* Socialists can admit no compromise with this aim, no scaling it down to 'a high and stable level of employment', no playing with the idea that 'a small dose of unemployment' might be good for production. Just as the certainty of a job is the first condition of decent living, so is full employment the first condition of a socialist economy. Even if it could be proved conclusively – and all the evidence points in the opposite

---

* Full employment cannot, of course, mean zero unemployment. At any moment there will always be some workers unemployed, as they change from one job to another. What is meant is as many vacancies as there are unemployed.

direction – that a revival of the fear of unemployment would increase productivity, this would be a poor bargain and a disgraceful exchange.

But the very achievement of full employment has raised a new problem of economic security – the problem of 'creeping inflation'. There has been a continual rise in the cost of living, and even though inflation may not be so disastrous in its effects as unemployment, its consequences are serious enough. It may be a boon to speculators, to the owners of real property or to the businessmen for whom rising prices mean rising profits, but it means anxiety and hardship for many whose incomes are fixed or low. Social incomes and small personal savings are devalued. The trade unions must spend their energies on constant wage claims to do no more than maintain real wages. In industries, where there is strong resistance to an increase in prices, strikes occur and further insecurity results.

Full employment without inflation is, then, the general condition for economic security. How to plan for it is now familiar ground; it is primarily a matter of controlling demand. General unemployment is due to an inadequate total demand, known, in the customary language of the inter-war years, as 'under-consumption' or 'over-production' depending on your point of view. General inflation is due to an excessive total demand; or, in the popular phrase of to-day, 'too much money chasing too few goods'. The responsibility of governments is to regulate demand so that it is neither too small nor too large for the existing supply of goods.

The main controls over the general level of demand are the banks and the budget. Through the banks the government can regulate the supply of money by varying the rates of interest at which they lend; in this way – by making money dear or cheap – the total volume of demand can be contracted or expanded. But continual changes in interest rates in themselves introduce new insecurities in the economy. In any case they provide both an inadequate and an indiscriminate instrument of control. The control is inadequate because when demand is buoyant, dear money will not necessarily deter the borrower; and when demand is slack, cheap money will not necessarily induce him to spend. It is indiscriminate because – so far as it is successful – it contracts or expands all borrowing, regardless of the social implications. House-purchase is discouraged at the same time as hire-purchase, investment in necessities no less than investment in luxuries. And, as the control affects spending out of borrowed money only, it always cuts down investment rather than consumption. The government may support the changes in interest rates by directing the credit policies of the banks, thus putting on their shoulders the responsibility of discrimination. But they are not equipped with either the information or the experience to apply the priorities arising out of a national economic policy.

The budget is a much more direct and effective instrument for controlling general demand. The government can vary the volume of demand by taxing more or less than it spends, that is by running a surplus or a deficit in the nation's accounts. It can do more than this. Through discriminatory taxation it can influence different forms of spending. Direct taxation can distinguish in its effects between rich and poor, between personal spending and spending on investment. Indirect taxation can distinguish between spending on particular goods.

Before the war, the problem was to sustain a sagging general demand which led to unemployment; since the war it has been to restrict a buoyant demand leading to inflation. This second problem has remained unresolved, not because the budget could not deal with it, but because governments have failed to use the budget resolutely enough. Increased taxation is the obvious means for reducing excessive expenditure, but governments have been unwilling to face the strong political opposition which new taxation invokes, or even to resist the continuous pressure for less taxation. No government has been ready to incur the unpopularity of putting four-square to the public the case for weighting the burden of taxation yet further. The alternative would be to reduce its own expenditure, but what it spends on defence or on social services, for example, should be determined by quite other considerations.

This is one of the great tests of statesmanship in a fully-employed economy. Is a government willing to resist the pressures of immediate interests for the sake of an overall security? The Labour government certainly showed a far greater readiness to meet the test than successive Conservative governments have done. It was more prepared to uphold the high rate of taxation and to enforce stringency, whereas the Conservatives have tended to reduce taxation and rely rather on high interest rates and a policy of tight money, with all its weaknesses and lack of discrimination.

But the problem does not end there. Full employment without inflation cannot be secured only from the side of demand; sometimes supply must also be controlled. When changes in demand are gradual, supply adjusts itself to them without serious disolocation. But when there are rapid and large shifts in demand, then specific shortages or surpluses in supply may occur for particular products. These may not create a condition of general insecurity in any way comparable with the fluctuations of the trade cycle, but they do create insecurity for those affected. Surpluses will throw men out of work, and shortages will push up prices.

The remedial action which can be taken is well known. Shortages may, for example, be dealt with by physical controls; surpluses may be temporarily absorbed by government buying and stockpiling. These controls are no permanent solution, although it is usually better to resort to them than to allow the dislocation to spread. They are not, as is far too often assumed, the essence of planning; rather are they the consequences of its neglect or imperfections.

By far the better way of dealing with the surpluses and shortages which lead to specific unemployment and specific inflation – and this may more properly be called planning – is for the government to try to foresee changes in the structure of demand and to take advance action to change supply accordingly. To foresee changes means very much better methods of statistical forecasting than we possess at present; to take advance action means the introduction of planning into a different field – the planning of production. Nothing like a detailed production plan for every industry is required, what is needed is the deliberate expansion of the industries where shortages are occurring and which are likely to enjoy a growing demand, and the orderly contraction of others where demand is likely to decline.*

The key to the planning of production is the planning of investment; here we are still only at the beginning of our experience. Something can be done through financial controls. The banks, for example, may be given directives to whom to lend, and capital issues can be controlled. But these methods, at best, will only be partially effective. They may encourage investment in some industries and discourage it in others by making funds more easy or more difficult of access, but there is no guarantee that the industries for whom the funds are available will in fact undertake the investment on a large enough scale, or that industries which are determined to expand will not find the funds to do so, not least from their own undistributed profits.

This is why financial controls must be supported by more direct government controls over investment. The most effective direct restriction on investment is the licensing of new buildings, for what is licensed is homogeneous and visible and therefore most susceptible to supervision. But any control which allocates physical resources can do no more than prevent people from investing contrary to gov-

* Apart from war and armaments, the main reasons for large shifts in demand are changes in foreign trade, either temporary fluctuations or long-term changes in the pattern of trade. It is particularly difficult to forecast these changes, since they depend on the policies of other governments. The only satisfactory solution is international economic planning. But while that makes so little headway in the present world, we have to do the best we can within the national framework. For this reason alone, foreign trade and currency movements must continue to be controlled, or the economy would be completely at the mercy of external forces.

ernment plans. To fulfil the plan by positive action the best way is for the government itself to become the investor. Help in different forms has been given to some industries in the past; oil-refining and aircraft, for example. But except for nuclear power, direct government investment in civilian industries is very rare. There is no reason whatsoever why it should remain so. On the contrary, this is a most valuable and important planning instrument.

Perhaps the most difficult problem of production planning in a democracy is to secure an orderly contraction of industries which cannot hope to sustain their past production. The textiles industry is the most obvious illustration in this country. There is bound to be strong political resistance to contraction from all those connected with industry – workers no less than employers. But apart from this, the industry cannot be denied all new investment and allowed to languish in increasing inefficiency. What is needed, rather, is to concentrate production in its most efficient units. This means selective investment, not to enlarge production generally, but to ensure that what is produced is produced economically. A strict government control of investment is needed, undertaken in conjunction with schemes for concentration prepared by the industry itself. The government has to use its power in order to compel the industry to face the facts of its own future.

Wage-Price Spiral

Most of the controls needed for dealing with fluctuations in supply and demand have existed in this country; certainly no drastic increase in the powers of government is called for. Apart from restoring a few controls which have been abandoned, what is particularly needed is the cultivation of foresight regarding the trends, and the forging of a political will to use to the full the instruments already at hand. But now, in a fully-employed economy a new source of insecurity has arisen; one which cannot be dealt with by any of these established methods.

It arises from the constant pressures on every side for increased incomes. Those who are in the strongest market positions, or who are most ruthless in exploiting their bargaining power, can assert their claims and hold the community to ransom. Every section of the community justifies its own demands by reference to the increases enjoyed by others. But each advance is a Pyrrhic victory for it forces the pace all round, and most of what is gained on the swings of increased incomes is lost on the roundabouts of increased prices. This is customarily called the wage-price spiral. 'It takes all the running you can do to keep in the same place,' as the Red Queen said to Alice.

It is not only the inflationary consequences of the wage-price spiral which create insecurity. This merry-go-round of competition for sectional advantage places a premium on the scramble for more money. Any stable basis for income relationships is destroyed; the community is split into hostile groupings. The security of the economy is once again endangered, to an accompaniment of increasing recrimination and industrial conflict.

Far from having a policy to meet this situation, many socialists have not even been prepared to discuss it candidly; they have shied away from doing as much as look it in the face. There are obvious reasons for this hesitation. The difficulty starts with the intense resistance of the trade unions against anything smacking of compulsory wage regulation. They want to be free to negotiate as they will. They are staunch adherents of the voluntary tradition in British industrial relations, on the basis of which they have developed their present forms and functions. And, indeed, there is much to be said for their view. It is only right that people should have a say in fixing their own incomes, and should be able to combine to better their lot. Governments are, anyway, not always to be trusted; nor would it be a good thing if every wage claim developed into a political battle between the unions and the government.

Even the proposal that the Trades Union Congress itself should have the power to arbitrate among the claims of the various unions meets with no sympathy, and again for understandable reasons. Every wage-claim would then become an inter-union battle, leading to disunity and endless friction among the workers themselves. This could only be avoided by a dangerous concentration of power in the hands of a few men at the top, who would themselves be put in an impossible position. And in one important respect the result would be the same as if the government intervened; the unions would lose that which they prized most – their own autonomy.

It is not only the unions who oppose any central regulation of wages; all these arguments are repeated from the other side of industry. The employers' federations, for their part, object no less to interference with their autonomy. They cling just as fiercely to their right, within each industry, to settle their own affairs. They, too, want no government intervention; they have not even established a single central body which can speak with the same authority as the Trades Union Congress. Many of them are particularly interested in retaining as much freedom as possible, in order to compete with each other for labour by offering higher wage-rates.

In dealing with wages regulation, two problems must be distinguished. There is the problem of wage and salary differentials as between different occupations and industries, and there is the problem of work incomes as a whole in relation to other personal incomes. With the first, we already have some experience to go on; there has been some ordering of wage structures within the limits of individual industries. One of the results of the growth of collective bargaining has been the setting up of Joint Industrial Councils and their like, and some of these have successfully graded the different occupations within the industry, the better to regulate the wage rates due to each. True, it has taken years of patient negotiation to eliminate many unnecessary and inequitable differentials, but it has been done. The building industry is a well-known example, and, more recently, a start has been made in working out a national wages structure for the extremely complicated case of coal-mining.

To press forward with a properly ordered wage structure in each industry is the first condition for curbing competitive bargaining; but there is no reason why the process should stop there. What is good for each industry can hardly be bad for the economy as a whole. Unions and employers have managed to get together on an industrial basis to eliminate barren competition, why should it be impossible for them to do so on a national scale? Government initiative would be required in calling together the central representatives of employers and trade unions. There need be no compulsion, and certainly no rigidity. Bargaining could be conducted freely; but it would be bargaining to introduce some intelligent and acceptable system into wage-rates, not bargaining for sectional advantage alone. What was agreed would not be fixed forever; it could be reviewed and adjusted every year. We do not deceive ourselves that this process, which sounds essentially simple on paper, would not be long and difficult in practice.* But a start has to be made, and what alternative is there which is likely to meet with success?

No government is likely to act until it is generally recognized that simplicity and stability in the national wage and salary structure would be a good thing. That point of understanding has not yet been reached. On the contrary, many still assert that what is wanted is greater flexibility, so that employers would have greater freedom to compete for labour by offering better wages. Labour would then go where it is most needed. That is, in the end, an argument for chaos. And chaos is the result in, for instance, the engineering industry, where the absence of any national joint

* One of the greatest complications arises out of the growing divergence between actual earnings and wage rates. The extent to which earnings are effectively regulated by collective agreement varies from industry to industry, but there has undoubtedly been an increase in the payments which agreements do not control. The attainment of an ordered wage structure will depend on the comprehensiveness of collective agreements in regulating all the elements which make up the paypacket and their strict observance in practice.

council for regulation has led to an increasingly haphazard wage structure. Earnings in different sections of the industry and in different parts of the country vary, and vary greatly, without rhyme or reason. The chaos spreads into other industries with better ordered wage structures, who find themselves short of workers in particular areas because of the high rates paid there by individual engineering employers.

There is, in fact, no evidence that day-to-day fluctuations in wage rates bring about a satisfactory re-distribution of labour. The movement of labour is more likely to be influenced by the availability of jobs and houses and by the provisions which are made for training and guiding new entrants. The control of wage competition does not prevent employers from attracting workers by improving working conditions and according their employees a higher status and better treatment. This is a better method than wage competition for maintaining the mobility of labour.

Once some order is brought into the national wage structure, it becomes possible to tackle the second problem, and for the government, trade unions, and employers to reach some agreement on wage movements as a whole in relation to the movement of other incomes. One thing is certain, wages cannot be dealt with separately. If they are to be stabilized, so must dividends, interest rates, and rents. The workers cannot be expected to restrict their demands when other and wealthier sections of the community are making hay while the sun shines. A national wages policy presupposes a national policy for the distribution of personal incomes as a whole. Such a policy cannot be based on the assumption that the present inequalities in income distribution are sacred. The advance towards stability must be accompanied by an advance towards equality. Even the limited aim of economic security cannot be achieved in isolation; it is necessarily bound up with the struggle for fair shares.

8

FAIR SHARES

The Fixing of Incomes

In a market economy, incomes depend on what people have to sell – it may be their services or the use of their property – and on what others are prepared to pay for it. What they have to sell varies greatly. Some have special capacities, perhaps unique gifts; some own much more property than others; some are simply born lucky – they have the gambler's flair. Equally, what people are prepared to pay bears no relation to the seller's efforts or needs. A sleeping-partner in a business may pocket several times the income of the highly trained engineer he employs; a confirmed bachelor with no responsibilities may be earning much more than the heavily-burdened family man. The market, in settling incomes, is indifferent to the demand for fair shares.

Incomes to-day, however, are not left entirely to the free play of the market. To some extent they are regulated by organization. Workers are organized in trade unions which bargain for better wages; professional people have their associations to defend their interests; employers band together both to present a united front in wage-negotiations and to control their prices and, indirectly, their profits. The government also intervenes. It protects the wages of weakly-organized workers and supports voluntary regulation in various ways; it exerts some influence in fixing the wages and salaries of its own employees; it determines interest rates; and through price controls it has, on rare occasions, cut down profits. But all these attempts to regulate must take the market conditions of supply and demand into account. In any case, their result is not always a greater measure of equality; it may merely reflect the strength of superior organization or the exploitation of a monopoly position.

Why, it is asked, should the government not take on itself the task of settling all incomes, and so do away with the injustices of the market? We have already shown how difficult it is to set up quantitive criteria for fair shares, and to fix all incomes accordingly. The more one considers the complex circumstances of individual lives, the more impossible it appears to work out exactly what in justice is due to each. We have also argued that state regulation of all incomes is undesirable because it would involve drastic inroads into personal freedom, and turn every claim for a wage or salary increase into a nation-wide political battle.

Redistribution of Incomes

The method which has in fact been chosen to bring some fairness into the distribution of incomes is an entirely different one – the method of taxation. The market makes its decisions, which means that some get much more than others. Then the government steps in and proceeds to tax away a good part of the difference. This is now the accepted practice of all British governments – and most others as well. Even the post-war Labour government, when it made a radical departure from tradition by publishing its *Statement on Personal Incomes, Costs and Prices* in 1948, was careful to begin by recognizing that it was not desirable for it 'to interfere directly with the incomes of individuals other than by taxation'.

Income tax has so far proved to be the best instrument for cutting away income differences. It is nicely flexible; it can be graduated steeply, so that the higher the income the higher the rate at which it is taxed; it can be relaxed to allow for special needs. As a result of generations of stiff income-taxing, the gap between the extremes of wealth and poverty has been narrowed in this country. Something like a national maximum of net income (that is, income after taxation) has been established. To retain much more than this, so very much more has to be earned – because most of the extra will be taxed away – that very few can manage it.

Out of the revenue gained by taxation, the government has been able to build up what amounts to a national minimum at the other end of the scale. All sorts of 'social incomes' are distributed – pensions, family allowances, national assistance, sickness benefits and so on – which between them go a long way to ensure that everyone has at least the minimum on which to live.

Although the tax system thus evolved could be simplified and improved – and many detailed proposals have been made – it is doubtful if further radical changes in income distribution could be effected by tax methods alone. Why not? Because allowing people to make unjustifiably high incomes and then cutting them down by taxation carries with it serious disadvantages.

One disadvantage – so it is sometimes asserted – is that high direct taxation weakens monetary incentives. This argument is usually exaggerated, because it is too easily assumed that the only incentive to work is a cash reward; reduce the reward by taxation and, on this assumption, people will work less hard, be less energetic and less enterprising. Whether the result is indeed so, has never been proved; there are, in fact, many other incentives to work which operate regardless of earnings. Yet as long as the money motive remains so important in our economy, this possible drawback to high taxation cannot simply be ignored.

The main drawback is evasion, and it is one which has been assuming dangerous proportions since the war. Illegal tax evasion, it is true, is not very widespread in this country as compared, say, with some of our continental neighbours. Because of this respect for the law, income tax has become so powerful an instrument of redistribution here. But legal tax dodges are nevertheless rife. They account for millions of pounds every year in spite of the continual tightening up of tax laws and administration. As soon as one loophole is stopped the rich tax-payer, for whom large sums are at stake, employs a tax accountant to find or devise another.

The most common form of legal tax evasion is the reckless use of business expense accounts in private industry. These are now often worth substantially more to those in a position to claim them than the salaries they are paid. The procurement of cars for the family, car running expenses, lavish entertainment allowances, conferences abroad which happen to coincide with holidays, can all escape the tax inspector's net.

Apart from these methods of dodging the tax-collector, there is the big loophole of tax-free capital gains. The distribution of bonus shares, take-over bids, the financial reconstruction of companies, the formation of holding and subsidiary companies and many other complicated manipulations are employed by the rich to get richer. The government is always fighting a battle of wits, in which it is by no means always the winner; and the higher the taxation the greater the incentive to devise ways for getting round it.

Given the will to take them, there are obvious measures for tightening up our existing tax legislation. If it is necessary to allow firms to get their business by competing with each other in lavish entertainment at the public expense, surely they should be subject to the strictest scrutiny, so that the abuses which are common knowledge to-day may be averted. This can be done by strengthening the tax inspectorate in numbers and power, so that they can and do ask more questions. If tax is being evaded by converting profits into capital gains, there is a strong case for supplementing income tax by a capital gains tax, such as already exists in the United States. In some cases, we know, it is unfair to tax away capital gains; there is the house-owner, for example, who sells his house for three times what he paid twenty years ago, but who will need the whole of this sum to buy a new residence. But this is only a reason for making the right exceptions.

To stop the loopholes in income-tax legislation is important, but under high direct taxation some are always bound to persist. Indirect taxes – that is, taxes on what one buys (e.g. purchase tax or tobacco duty) paid in the form of a higher price – are not open to this objection. Indeed, they have certain advantages. They do not weaken incentives; they are more difficult to evade; they are easier to administer. What is more, they are a valuable instrument in planning, because the demand for particular products can be influenced by the rate of tax imposed on them. But they have their disadvantages too. They raise prices and so encourage inflation. The main socialist objection to indirect taxation has been that it does not vary according to income, so that given an unequal income distribution, it burdens the poor more than the rich. Unless it is imposed only on the luxuries of the wealthy, which would not suffice to raise the revenues we need, it has the fault of making injustice more unjust.

Taxing incomes for fair shares always runs into this difficulty of the heavy inequalities at the source. Because wealth is so unevenly distributed, people are permitted to draw very unequal gross incomes. If we try to eliminate these by high direct taxation, we run into all the problems of trying to lop off bits here and there in order to add them on elsewhere. The result is a complicated income tax system, replete with anomalies and engendering the most troublesome administrative and psychological problems. If we follow the method of indirect taxation, the result is to penalize most those who are already most penalized. The obvious solution to these dilemmas is to get rid of the inequalities at the source.

Redistribution of Property

There are two main reasons why the distribution of incomes is so grossly unequal at the source. The first is the great disparities in the ownership of property; a small fraction of the population own so large a part of the nation's wealth that they are bound to draw large unearned incomes simply because of the size of their holdings. The second is that certain types of property, notably the ownership of business enterprise, yield a high return in the form of distributed profits and capital gains. Not only do the owners of the ordinary shares in these private concerns derive substantial incomes from them, but the profits permit the payment of very high salaries to the leading managerial posts and the granting of extravagant allowances in the form of expense accounts. These two reasons for the persistently heavy income inequalities continually reinforce each other on the principle of 'to him that hath more shall be given'. High profits swell the unearned incomes derived from past accumulations of property, and in turn provide the basis on which new accumulations are built.

At first glance there may seem to be a simple solution to this problem. Why should the state not intervene to redistribute property, as it redistributes incomes, with the aim of allowing everyone to possess a fairly equal share? This is not a practical policy. In principle there is nothing against the widest possible spread of property over the whole population; the desire to own, to save, and to bequeath is a natural and, within limits, justified human interest. But people's attitudes towards property vary so much that even if a fair distribution were secured at any moment, it would not remain so for long. Some would immediately turn their holdings into cash and spend them; others would use them for accumulating more. Some would neglect whatever possessions they had, others would maintain and treasure them. There is certainly a case for the government to help those who want to acquire something of their own – house-ownership is an obvious example, or assistance to the small businessman or farmer – but no one has seriously suggested that the big private fortunes should be parcelled out and given away as presents to the propertyless.

Instead, socialists have looked to a solution through transferring the large accumulations from private to public ownership. Once in public hands, so it is argued, then all the income – whether in the form of rent, interest, or profit – would come to the benefit of the whole community instead of being concentrated to the advantage of a fortunate minority. Capital gains, too, would flow into public hands, and the creation of new private accumulations made increasingly difficult.

The method of transfer which has so far been most favoured, and which has figured largest in socialist propaganda, has been the nationalization of industry. But ten years' experience has revealed how little nationalization can contribute to a rapid advance towards fair shares. It is impossible, within a democracy, to nationalize without compensating the existing owners. That would cause so much injustice that the consent of the electorate is hardly likely to be given. It would be totally unfair to expropriate some groups of owners, including many small-holders who might lose all their savings just because they had happened to invest in an industry suitable for nationalization, while others, with no claim to privileged treatment, were allowed to get off scot free because they had had the luck to invest elsewhere.

Once it has been agreed to pay compensation, nationalization becomes nothing other than compulsory purchase of property by the state; its immediate result is not a redistribution but the exchange of one form of property for another. The shares held in the former private companies are exchanged for fixed-interest-bearing government bonds. The exchange is not without its long-term significance, providing the industry is an expanding and prosperous one, because the bond-holders receive only a fixed interest instead of sharing in rising profits and capital gains and so being able to build up new accumulations. But there is nothing to prevent the bond-holders selling them and investing the proceeds in the profitable enterprise still in private hands. It is only in the long run, as more and more industries are nationalized, that the whole basis for private property accumulations becomes narrowed and a real redistribution of wealth results.

The only way to effect an immediate change in the distribution of property by methods acceptable to a democracy, is for the government to levy property away on a graduated basis, taking proportionately more from the larger than from the smaller holdings. There is, in fact, nothing revolutionary about this idea; something of the sort is already being done by death duties. But with one very important difference; death duties in their present form are a tax on the property bequeathed rather than a levy, they transfer money and not the property itself. They are paid in cash and treated by the government as an addition to current revenue. Property may be sold to pay the duties, but it is sold to some other property-owner so that the overall distribution between the public and the private sectors remains more or less unchanged.

To increase the proportion of public ownership, death duties must be made payable in kind or securities, or else the cash must not be spent but used by the government to purchase new property. This is a reform of fundamental importance. But even death duties as at present levied, permit of serious loopholes; the most obvious is the opportunity to dispose of property in gifts before death. If the duties are to be more effective in redistributing property, this practice has to be stopped, and the rates at which they are imposed, stiffened. There is no reason why a maximum should not be fixed for all wealth transmitted to heirs and everything above taxed one hundred per cent.

Even then, death duties would remain slow in their working, as only a small proportion of private property becomes liable for duty each year. They are at best a gradual method for correcting the heritage of capitalist accumulation. The quicker method would be a once-for-all capital levy, by which the government would take over all private property holdings above a fixed maximum – without waiting for the owner to die. Even if the maximum were put as high as £10,000 and only everything above that figure were levied away, the government would at once acquire more than half the nation's total private wealth.

Why, then, do socialists hesitate to advocate a capital levy on this scale? No valid objection can be raised against it on ethical grounds, and the administrative difficulties are by no means insuperable. The real obstacles are political.

Popular consent would have to be won before such a drastic measure could be introduced. Indeed, the choice between reformed death duties and a capital levy, or possibly some combination of both, must always depend on what is politically possible. The pace of the advance towards fair shares within a democracy, as with every other socialist objective, is ultimately governed by what the electorate will permit.

Whatever progress is made in these ways, they serve only to alter the existing distribution of property. But the situation we are dealing with is not a static one. New property is constantly being acquired out of new savings, and even if the existing situation were revolutionized, new disparities in ownership would soon emerge. To maintain a different ratio between public and private ownership, there must also be a different ratio between public and private savings. If the public sector of the future is to be relatively greater, then public savings must now exceed private. Under the Labour government such a trend was in fact established; it has been reversed by the Conservatives.

Public saving may take place in two ways – through the surpluses of income over outgoings earned by public enterprises, or through the surpluses of public revenue over public expenditure, raised by taxes. Looked at from the point of view of the need for increased public savings, the present financial policy imposed on the nationalized industries is nonsensical. They are expected to do no more than balance their accounts, taking the good years with the bad, while borrowing out of private savings in order to finance their capital development. Why should not public enterprise provide for its own development by running a surplus in the same way as private enterprise does, and so directly increase the proportion of public savings, instead of increasing the proportion of private? There is a similar case for the government, and the local authorities, to pay for as much as possible of their capital equipment out of their own revenue rather than having continually to pay interest to private investors.

But once the government enters the field as a large-scale property-owner, another question arises. What property should it acquire? The proceeds of death duties in kind or of a capital levy will consist of a heterogeneous collection of land, buildings, and securities. Which is it to retain, and which to sell, and what will it purchase in exchange? The same questions apply to public savings. Though they may be used mainly to finance developments in the public industries or to provide for the government's own capital expenditure, they could also be used to acquire new property. We mentioned at the outset that some forms of property yield high profits and are thus a continual source of unequal incomes. Is it this type of property that should be acquired, so that the high profits will accrue to the government and not to private individuals?

Proposals have been put forward that the government might buy up a proportion of the shares in prosperous concerns rather than nationalize them entirely. The public would thus be able to reap all the benefits of lucrative revenues and participation in the capital gains, without incurring the heavy responsibilities of administration. But there are dangers in this tempting course. The government would acquire a vested interest in maintaining the high profits, thus lending countenance to high profits – with all the inequalities that flow from them – in other industries as well.

When the state participates in industry it must do so, not merely to increase its revenue, but with the whole of its economic policy in mind. In the interest of fair shares one of its aims must be to reduce easy profits. High profit margins may sometimes be justified as a compensation for the risks of genuine pioneering enterprise. But the great bulk of high profits do not come from adventurous experiments in industry. On the contrary, they are gained in secure and established concerns enjoying a high degree of monopoly. These are the entrenched positions of privilege within the community which can only be subjected to public attack by the government as an outright owner, controlling the policy of a variety of business enterprise within its ownership.

The attack may be mounted in different ways. The complete nationalization of a particular industry is only one of them. An industry may be partially nationalized by the government taking over one or more firms within it, thus enabling public enterprise to break price rings by competing directly with private enterprise. Or bulk buying by public agencies can be used to bring pressure to bear on prices and reduce profits. More will be achieved from the point of view of fair shares by public intervention in any of these ways, than by the part purchase of high-yielding shares, or by the still less effective method of nationalizing bankrupt industries.

But the role cast for public ownership cannot be determined only by the aim of fair shares. There are other reasons which will determine its extension and the form it should take. Not least among these are the requirements of an expanding economy.

9
EXPANDING ECONOMY

It is rare for capitalists to deliver a frontal attack on the socialist demand for fair shares. Their opposition is usually argued not on the grounds of principle but of expediency. Fair shares, they say, can only be had at the cost of economic stagnation. 'Your egalitarian policies', they assert, 'will sap the sources of economic expansion. Expansion depends, firstly, on adequate investment. By equalizing incomes and so reducing the savings of the rich, you will diminish the possibilities of capital accumulation. The nation will consume more and save less; so there is less available for new investment. Secondly, expansion depends on the pressure of competition; every industrialist is kept on his toes by the rivalry of his competitors. But in the interests of equality you ask the government to interfere with the market and introduce nation-wide public monopolies. The force of competition will be weakened and nothing so effective substituted in its place. Thirdly, expansion depends on monetary incentives. But you, in the name of equality, want to tax the fruit of enterprise and the reward of hard work to such an extent that money incentives will lose their force. What alternative do you offer?' These are challenges which must be met. What is the socialist answer?

The Role of Investment

Under nineteenth-century capitalism the problem of savings looked after itself. Indeed it looked after itself so competently that there was more to invest than people knew what to do with. Capital had to compete for outlets; because there were insufficient outlets at home capitalists were attracted to imperialist adventures abroad. Capital accumulated so rapidly because wealth was so badly distributed. The rich had rapidly growing fortunes to dispose of;

however much they spent on their personal needs, plenty still remained for investment. So they invested yet more and became yet richer.

To-day all this has changed. The rich are less rich and the poor less poor, and neither has much of a surplus to save out of their incomes. The problem is not to find outlets for capital to fill, but to find the capital to fill the outlets. Demand is rising everywhere. Overseas territories are crying out for capital, which does not come forward. All the pressures are on the side of more and immediate personal consumption. Governments have increasing difficulty in resisting this demand; investment easily becomes the residual claimant, to be cut whenever the pressure of consumers' demand becomes too powerful.

This is a new dilemma. But the socialist answer to it is not to sacrifice the dearly-won advance towards equality. They have no desire to return to the days when the rich were permitted to go on amassing capital and investing it with continuing profit to themselves. On the contrary, in their eyes this situation demands resolute government action. Only the government can represent the interests of the community as a whole and protect it – and future generations as well – against the immediate and short-sighted demands of sectional interests.

There are three sources of savings: personal, business, and governmental. The government cannot tell people what their personal savings should be; and even if it could this source is now inadequate. Its place has been taken increasingly by business savings which come out of the undistributed profits of industry. If savings are to increase still further, the argument now runs, industry must be allowed to maintain high profits. But high private profits lead to an accentuation of inequality. Even if they are undistributed, they cause a rise in the value of ordinary shares, and the growth of those large property accumulations, which is precisely what socialists would like to see eliminated. Of course, in the case of public enterprise, these objections to high profits do not hold. If the nationalized industries built up surpluses of their own, they could create important new sources of savings. At present, however, they do not do so because they are expected to break even in their accounts, and they look to the capital market or to direct government assistance for new investment. But even if this irrational policy were abandoned, it is obvious that these industries alone could not meet the nation's needs.

To secure all the necessary savings, we must, then, rely on their third source – government saving. How is this done? The government can compel the nation to save by taxing away sufficient of private incomes to build up budget surpluses, which means that it taxes more than it spends. This is an equitable way of saving, leading through graduated taxation to greater equality rather than to greater inequality. It is more conducive to industrial peace, for wage-earners are not asked to exercise restraint while property-owners pile up their fortunes. But politically it is more difficult. The consent of the electorate has to be gained. People must understand why the savings are necessary, and be willing to support a policy which involves the sacrifice of some immediate consumption for the sake of a better future.

In totalitarian countries, all the savings needed can be raised without difficulty by government action, because the consent of the people is not required. In a democracy the government has to win a willing co-operation. It has to explain why savings are needed to finance investment. A visible investment plan must be presented to the nation so that the purposes of their sacrifices can be made clear to all. The government must show how it intends to use its investment funds. It must show, too, the necessity for investment planning. The nation is concerned not only to find capital for the immediately profitable projects which are usually able to find sufficient funds anyhow, but with many other developments which have difficulty in raising finance. If investment is left to private individuals or businesses, it will naturally be put to the uses which will bring them the greatest return. It may take no account of the overall national needs.

The investment which requires public stimulation is broadly of four kinds. First, in industries which are vital to the community but which may not, for various reasons, attract the private investor. The railways are an obvious example. Private capital prefers the certainty of a good return from investment in, say, motor-cars. The result is that the roads are swamped with motor-cars, but we continue to put up with an inefficient, squalid, and out-of-date – though vitally necessary – railway system. Public investment is, secondly, necessary for the development of new industries to which heavy risks are attached and for which very large capital resources are required. Nuclear power is a case in point, where development has already depended on government initiative and investment.

A third and different aspect of public investment is for industrial research and training – for increasing the nation's technical knowledge and capacities so that productivity may be raised. Private enterprise can scarcely be expected to cope with this, except in successful highly-profitable industries which can afford to set aside large sums for long-term purposes. The industries which are most in need of 'know-how' are those least likely to afford the new knowledge which is their hope of salvation.

Finally – and very important – public investment is required in all those social amenities and services which raise the quality of life for every citizen. Education, health, housing, roads, community services in their broadest sense, all fall in this category. These are never likely to be a paying proposition. Unless public authorities direct investment into them, they will always be starved of funds. Capital will flow into the provision of the marketable goods, but not into the services which give the life of the community a richer content. Where is the sense in cheeseparing on the whole environment in which people live, and in which children grow to maturity, while capital is being poured into the manufacture of luxury goods and more capital has to be thrown after it in advertising to induce people to buy this plethora of wares?

To assert that the individual is robbed of his free choice of products if investment is planned by the government, is no argument. To-day free choice applies mainly to the range of goods that some manufacturer finds it profitable to produce. If people are to be able to broaden their range of choice, then profit cannot be the sole criterion for investment. Many of the most socially desirable investments will never pay their way. They will never take place at all unless society insists.

Spurs to Efficiency

To plan and apportion the resources of the community so that sufficient is devoted to investment and the total divided among all the necessary investment projects, is the first condition of an expanding economy. But what is to ensure that industrial production, which is the basis of economic expansion, will be efficient? Under capitalism, this was said to be the role of free competition. But under socialism, so it is argued, the state takes over; it co-ordinates smaller firms into nation-wide monopolies. Prices are no longer determined by the market, but fixed by boards or tribunals. There is no incentive to keep down costs and prices, to improve products, to struggle for sales. The market pressures which forced capitalists to be efficient, bold, and enterprising will have vanished.

But look at the facts. Even in private industry operating in a free market, something seems to have gone wrong with competition as a recipe for economic progress. We all know that firms survive which are neither enterprising nor efficient. We have often been told how great is the gap even within the same industry between the good firm and the bad one; yet the bad live on notwithstanding. The sluggishness of whole sections of private British industry has been emphasized time and again. The coal industry under private enterprise was for a generation a byword for stagnation, just as some sections of the textiles industry are to-day, in spite of their being competitive.

The fact is that the perfect competition of which some economists have dreamed was never more than an abstraction. In the real world it did not and could not exist. Labour and capital and demand have never been sufficiently mobile for choice to switch automatically from the worse to the better firm. Such competition as there was has never succeeded in eliminating every inefficient enterprise. On the contrary, it was often wasteful, each firm duplicating the same services and spending money to cut its rivals' throats. If there are too many competing firms, all are so busy struggling to survive that few may have the resources to modernize and innovate.

Yet, in spite of imperfections, competition is undoubtedly a spur to enterprise. But to-day – under the impact of increasing mechanization and large-scale production – competition is having difficulty in surviving at all. Even under unhampered capitalism, everything favours the trend towards monopoly, and even where there is not a nation-wide monopoly, local or regional monopolies are often found dominating the market. It may be no more than a bus company in a provincial town or a laundry service in a rural area, but in either case the heavy cost of equipment, the obvious economies to be had from controlling the whole demand, make it less and less likely that rivals will appear. To restore competitive conditions in many industries has become impossible in the face of modern techniques and requirements, all pressing in the opposite direction.

What is to be done? Problems sometimes create their own solutions, and monopolies – so it is said – create counter-monopolies. Competition may be crushed, but the powerful manufacturing combine now faces the equally powerful distributive combine. According to recent theories, competition is being replaced by 'countervailing power'. The consumer may no longer be able individually to protect himself by taking his custom elsewhere, but mass wholesalers and chain stores and consumers' co-operative societies now take up the cudgels on his behalf in order to increase their own trade. Trade unions also compel the large firms to be efficient, by their constant pressure for higher wages.

All this is true, but it is not a sufficient answer. There is nothing certain about the working of 'countervailing power'. The large distributor may be in league with the large manufacturer, each taking their rake-off from higher prices. A trade union may strike a bargain with an employer at the expense of the consumer. Countervailing power, like competition, does not provide an automatic mechanism to ensure efficiency.

The traditional socialist answer to this problem has been that the pressure of organized public opinion would replace the pressure of competition. Once an industry is taken into public ownership, it can be made by law to submit itself to public accountability in one form or another. Parliament will scrutinize its accounts, consumers' councils will watch over prices and service, workers will be brought on to consultative committees which will advise on conditions in the workshops. Just because an industry is large and publicly owned, its behaviour will be constantly in the public eye.

How does this work out in practice? We already know, from our experience of the nationalized industries, how difficult it is to make accountability really effective, and to create an active and informed public opinion. Even if it were effective, public opinion is by its nature a two-edged sword. It may discourage waste; it may insist on a fair deal for the worker; it may demand a high quality product. But it may also be fearful of risk; it may frown on experiments involving public money; it may hesitate too long before sanctioning a plunge. Public accountability encourages rectitude, but it may inhibit flexibility and experiment.

The fact is that none of these three external pressures to which industry may be subjected – competition, countervailing power, or public accountability – is effective in every circumstance. Each has its merits and its drawbacks, and all are needed so that, where one does not operate effectively, it can be supplemented by the other. The problem varies from industry to industry according to the scale of production, the nature of the product and the other factors which determine industrial organization. In one industry there may be too much and in another too little competition. There is no general panacea. All that is certain is that government action of various kinds is required to bring each of these pressures into full play.

Many proposals have already been made – but few followed with determination – for this sort of government actin. Sometimes competition needs to be restored, where its restriction is only intended to safeguard privilege and obstruct innovation. Government intervention for this purpose may range from legislation to prohibit restrictive practices to the setting up of competing public enterprise; it may also encourage co-operatives or municipalities or even rival firms to break the ring by providing them with the necessary capital. On the other hand, competition may be taken to excess, with the consequence of inefficiency and waste. Government action is then needed to integrate the industry. This was the idea behind the proposal for Development Councils, that they could provide common services for the industry – access to capital, research and marketing arrangements which would be beyond the resources of individual firms. Despite their lack of success, due primarily to the resistance of trade associations and government reluctance in face of it, the need for this type of organization continues.

The use of public enterprise as countervailing power is still largely unexplored. The existing Public Corporations have very considerable purchasing powers which could be used deliberately as a pressure on suppliers to keep down their prices and improve their quality. Public enterprise could be extended with advantage into wholesale trade. Wholesaling is the strategic point from which countervailing power can be brought to bear on producers who are not under strong pressure of competition. In this way the government can come to the defence of individual consumers by concentrating their purchases.

But what pressures can be exerted on public enterprise itself? If it is subject to the checks of competition and countervailing power, there is no special problem. But where for technical reasons the whole of an industry is brought under public ownership public accountability must be the principal method of control. We already have some experience of accountability in the nationalized industries; it cannot be said that Parliament has yet found the ways of making it effective.

The difficulties are familiar. There is the dual danger of the government doing either too little or too much. A parliamentary debate once a year on the Annual Report cannot possibly suffice. On the other hand what has to be avoided is the hostile, petty criticism to which the Public Corporations are often submitted – peering over the shoulders of administrators, pillorying day-to-day decisions, calling attention to the risks which did not bear fruit and ignoring those that did. What is wanted is a reasonably objective and expert appraisal of the performance of public industry at longish intervals. A basis for fair criticism must be provided without crippling the initiative and responsibility of those in charge.

Not that the pressure of public accountability should be applied exclusively to public enterprise. Private enterprise can never be made fully accountable to the public, but there can be a limited accountability. The government, for example, can institute consumers' advisory services. Their value would lie not only in the assistance they could give to the consumer in making an informed choice, but in the pressure of public opinion on firms who, by skilful advertising, foist an expensive or inferior product on the public. Few firms of any size are indifferent to their public reputation, and it is a government responsibility to see that reputations are not gained on false pretences.

Apart from government action, the co-operative movement provides an interesting object lesson in the use, by the same organization, of all the three pressures – competition, countervailing power, and accountability. Co-operative societies compete in a big way with private enterprise in their services to the consumer. They also, through their extensive purchasing powers, could exert a countervailing power to the power of manufacturers and the producers of food and raw materials. Within their own organization, they have introduced a structure of accountability to their members unmatched in other enterprise, whether private or public. They possess, because of their large membership and widespread influence, great potentialities for influencing the economy as a whole.

It is common knowledge that these potentialities are by no means realized. The arrangements for accountability work feebly, because too few members are interested. In smaller towns the co-operative store often acquires something approaching a trading monopoly among the workers and loses correspondingly in efficiency. The societies may enter into league with manufacturers to maintain high prices, rather than exert their bargaining power against them. Where the co-operatives are most efficient is when all three controls come into action simultaneously – when accountability is supplemented by competition, and both are supplemented by the use of the whole movement's bargaining power to improve the lot of the consumer.

We have done no more than indicate the various ways of maintaining the pressures needed for an expanding economy. To go beyond this it would be necessary to analyse the structure and organization of each industry. But one conclusion stands out. Socialist thought – and for that matter capitalist thought – on the problems of industrial organization has been confused by too many unqualified approvals and condemnations. Both competition and monopoly have been the subject of attack, but neither is wholly bad nor wholly good. Similarly the antithesis of private versus public enterprise which treats the one as salvation and the other as damnation is too crude to be fruitful. What is clear, is that government action is necessary to keep industry under pressure to be efficient; the market of itself will not do it.

Motives for Work

Competition was only one half of the capitalist equation for securing an expanding economy; the other half was the money motive. Competition was thought to supply the external pressure; money the internal dynamic. Nineteenth-century conditions confirmed this belief in the driving-power of money. The man who ran an enterprise was often its owner; as the enterprise prospered so did he in direct proportion. The prospect of making a fortune within a lifetime was a powerful inducement to energy and initiative, especially to the self-made man who had known the rigours of poverty. Workers, on the other hand, were glad to have any job at all, and they expected to work hard to retain it; they were prepared to work harder still to earn a little more than the wretched minimum to which they were accustomed. There were few labour problems which the threat of the sack could not cure.

These conditions have changed. Heavy taxation has reduced the prospect of getting-rich-quick through industrial enterprise. The owner who prospered step by step with his business has been replaced, in all but the smaller concerns, by the manager on a fixed salary. Workers no longer need to be docile. A man can afford to choose now whether he wishes to work hard or not. Neither the carrot nor the stick is the inducement it used to be.

Why, then, should either managers or men give of their best to their work? If the compelling lure of money incentives has been weakened, what new dynamic can possibly take its place? The traditional socialist alternative was, of course, the motive of public service. Make industry the property of the community and everyone, so it was believed, would work with a will for the good of all. But is this really so? Already we have had enough experience of public enterprise to know that a change in ownership alone does not induce that kind of miracle. There are few people who can work continuously for some vague impersonal aim like 'the good of the community', even if they can be shown a direct connexion between their own seemingly insignificant efforts and the general welfare of their fellow-men. Motives in work, as in everything else, are usually more personal. In some way people must derive their own satisfactions from what they do.

Part of the satisfaction from work will always come from the income it brings. But the capitalist doctrine that people only work for the sake of money was false and misleading. Having been strongly propagated for more than a century, so much confusion has been created that it now requires intensive research by sociologists to rediscover the obvious – that people are also spurred on by other motives. It is not that nothing good is ever done for money, but it can be done for other reasons as well. The problem is not how to get rid of the money motive in the belief that everyone will then suddenly be inspired to work for the good of all. It is rather to recognize that under present circumstances the money motive is not enough and that other motives which give people the will to work must be liberated.

What is it, to-day, that gives the salaried manager the urge to be efficient and enterprising? His concern is, primarily, with his personal reputation; he wants to be esteemed for his success, to win recognition for his ability and his efforts and to be promoted to positions of higher esteem. But his personal reputation is bound up with the social reputation of his firm, and social reputations are made by society. If what society respects is the great industrial empire with the hard-headed business magnate at the top, then managers will strive to extend their power and their domain, without much care for the human consequences. If, on the other hand, society puts a premium on a courteous service to the public, on a high quality product, on good work relations, then a firm will gain its reputation by creating these, and they will become the goal of the manager's endeavours.

Management has now become, in essence, a profession like any other. It still lacks its formal professional ethic, but it is motivated in much the same way as the other professions. If a doctor is assured of a sufficient income, he devotes himself to his work not to earn more but for the sake of his reputation, for the satisfaction he gets from serving the community in a way the community appreciates. These are powerful motivations which the salaried manager already shares. Instead of deploring the waning strength of money incentives, there should rather be cause for rejoicing that material considerations need less and less dominate the lives of professional men. Instead they can give themselves to their work for much more deeply-satisfying reasons.

It is not so different in the case of the workers. Now that they are less compelled to work only for the sake of the pay-packet and to put up with any indignity, any degree of tedium, any misery which the job involves, the other motives, which people have always been ready to work for, can be released. People have always worked for the pride of honest achievement, for the pleasure of exercising a skill, for the satisfaction of working with mates in a team. The desire to enjoy one's work in all these ways is just as natural a motivation as the desire to increase one's income, once it becomes sufficient. But it is part of the perverseness of our society that this natural desire has been frustrated and suppressed.

Though workers do not have a public reputation to gain, as managers have, the personal esteem in which they are held by their colleagues in the workshop is for them, too, a matter of great concern. But what is it that the workshop esteems? That depends on the aims and methods both of management and of trade unions. If an industry is run, and the workers permit it, without regard to its effects on those who work in it, it places a premium on the rebel and the slacker – on active or passive protest. But if an industry is organized so as to value the man who uses his abilities, who is willing to share in consultation and to accept responsibility, then these are the qualities for which a worker will be esteemed, and which he will, consequently, feel the urge to cultivate.

A workshop which could draw forth all these virtues in its employees would of course be the manager's paradise.

Much of the current talk about good human relations in industry has precisely this in mind, for in this way – so it is hoped – productivity will be increased. But one essential factor is continually being missed. The spirit of responsibility and co-operation will not grow of itself, nor can it be created by moral appeals. The worker's attitude to his firm will depend on his firm's attitude to him. This leads straight to the problem of industrial democracy.

10
INDUSTRIAL DEMOCRACY

The life of man as producer is every bit as important as his
life as consumer. In theory people may assent; in practice
this fact is almost totally ignored. Industry makes no
attempt to strike a balance between its dual effects on man;
the producer is continually sacrificed to the product. It is
a remarkable comment on our present society that, despite
all the progress made in other directions, Aristotle's defini-
tion of a slave as a 'living tool' still remains a far too apt
description of the working life of the majority of industrial
employees.

The Political Parallel

The labour movement has had an answer to this problem –
industrial democracy. Just as democracy in the political
field has advanced the citizen towards equality, freedom,
and fellowship there, so it was believed that democracy in
industry would do the same for the worker in his work. But
although everyone is in favour of industrial democracy and
many fine words have been spoken about it, there is very
little agreement on what it really means. It represents a
deep-felt aspiration, rather than a guide to action. Resolu-
tions are passed in its favour, but no-one knows precisely
how to carry them out.

This was not always so. At one time there was no shortage
of plans and proposals, all based on the assumption that
industrial democracy meant transferring to industry the
successful methods of political democracy. In politics the
fundamental democratic device for enabling everybody to
assert his rights was the vote. With its aid the workers had
raised their status in society. They elected their own representatives to Parliament to look after their interests. They
had their own political party, the Labour Party, which was

going from strength to strength and would eventually take over the government of the country.

Why, then, should not the same course be followed in industry with the same results? There the worker also had the vote – within his trade union. As the unions increasingly brought all workers within their ranks and their power grew, they would be able to take over the control of industry and run it, through elected representatives, on democratic lines. Then, and then only, would the worker enter on his full rights and responsibilities. Industrial democracy was taken to be synonymous with workers' control.

There were, it is true, differences of opinion as to how this could be done with justice to all sections of the community. If industry were run by trade unions, who would protect the interests of the consumers? Out-and-out syndicalists thought this a red herring. How could the worker as producer, they asked, exploit himself as consumer? The guild socialists were not so glib; they recognized a real problem and insisted that it fell to the government to represent the consumers' interests in such matters as prices, as long as it did not interfere with the internal administration of industry. The labour movement as a whole, during the early twenties, favoured schemes for the joint control of industry whereby it would be run by representatives appointed both by the trade unions and by the government.

These ideas have now lost their appeal. Perhaps the most important reason is that the trade unions themselves, with few exceptions, no longer want to be responsible for the government of industry. They fear it would jeopardize their independence. They recognize that their first duty is to represent and protect the interests of their members, to act as their advocates. Once they participate in the government of industry they will be forced to consider many other things as well – the technical problems of production, the interests of the consumers, not to mention the position of the nation at large. Not only would they have to take this broader view – to some extent they do so already – but they would also be bound by the decisions which follow from it. They would no longer be free to voice their members' objections. Torn by conflicting loyalties, the union leaders would lose the confidence of their own ranks.

With the growing recognition of these dangers, other proposals for 'workers' control' have been canvassed. The trade unions, it is said, can continue to concentrate on their protective functions, but the workers in an enterprise could – quite independently of the unions – elect some or all of those in authority over them. Sometimes it is suggested that, as a first step, they should at least elect their foremen. Alternatively, it is proposed to start from the top and give the workers the right to elect a few of the directors of their firm, or, in the case of nationalized industries, some of the members of the boards.

One immediate objection to all these proposals is that the separation of the trade unions from the workers' managerial representatives, which they envisage, could not be sustained. The unions can hardly be expected to take kindly to any scheme which provides for elected representatives who would claim to interpret the workers' interests in rivalry with themselves. If such schemes were introduced against their will, which is hardly conceivable, they would be compelled in self-defence to make sure that their own nominees were elected. In this event the separation of functions would disappear and unions would, despite themselves, acquire managerial responsibilities.

This objection apart, what is misleading in all the various proposals for 'workers' control' is their assumption that the vote is the key to democracy in industry. Yet even in the political democracy which we have in this country, the expert administrators who run government departments, and who correspond to the managers in industry, are not elected. They are drawn from the Civil Service and reach their positions only after years of experience and special training. If they were elected, not only would the standards of administration fall, but the door would be opened to all kinds of jobbery and corruption. Exactly the same objections apply to the election of managers. The successful candidate would be the man who could win friends and court popularity; discipline and impartiality would be sacrificed in the struggle to win and keep votes.

In politics the voter does not even choose the ministers who compose the government; they are appointed by the leader of the party which has been elected into office. The significance of the vote is that it enables the individual elector to make a choice between alternative parties, so that all parties are compelled to respect his interests. To give the vote the same significance in industry it would be necessary to incorporate a party system into its administration, so that the worker could choose among rival programmes, and, if he wished, turn out the existing management if its performance fell short of his expectations. How industry could be successfully conducted in this way baffles the wildest of imaginations.

In any institutional sense the parallel between political and industrial democracy does not hold. It can only be drawn at a deeper level. The democratic idea is not tied to any particular set of arrangements for conducting human affairs. What democrats are really concerned about is to prevent those in authority from abusing their power, and to allow everyone to participate in making the decisions which affect him. The methods of achieving these aims, even in politics, vary in different parts of the world. There is no such thing as a model democratic constitution to which all countries should – or could – conform.

Similarly, what the advocates of industrial democracy have in mind is to find some arrangements which will curb the powers of managers and enable employees to have a say in what concerns them. The way to do this is not by imitating the methods of politics. Other methods must be sought, suited to industrial organization, which will yet secure the same result.

Achievements of Collective Bargaining

This is not a problem to which we come with a clean slate, but with generations of experience behind us. When the capitalist economic system first developed, employers wielded unbridled power over their employees. They no longer do so, for the very existence of strong trade unions deters employers from abusing their power. Workers are no longer helpless and alone; they can turn to their unions to deal with grievances in the knowledge that their fellow-workers stand behind them. With trade unions has come collective bargaining, which has not only strengthened the bargaining power of the workers, but has also done something more. It has introduced the 'rule of law' into industrial relations.

The collective agreements which result from negotiations set the norms for the individual contract of employment. The existence of these norms limits the power of the employer, because they are safeguarded by various sanctions, not least that of the strike. Unless the agreement is observed, employers are faced with the collective refusal of the workers to work. These voluntary agreements define the rights and obligations on both sides as effectively as by law. But with this great advantage – the law-making is less remote and more flexible than if it were the business of Parliament.

Collective bargaining obviously involves a balance of power between the two sides. Employers and employees both have keen, but often conflicting, interests in the terms agreed upon. If one side is much stronger than the other, the bargain arrived at will never be satisfactory for long. What first gave the workers their strength was organization, yet even organized employees cannot command a proper respect for their interests as long as employers can threaten them with life on the dole. Only when there is full employment can the two sides meet on fairly equal terms. Collective bargaining then becomes a very real measure of industrial democracy in the sense we have defined it.

True, the democratic achievements of collective bargaining are still only partial. So far efforts have been focused on the regulation of wages, hours of work, and kindred subjects. It is more the exception than the rule – at least

outside public employment – for other aspects of the con
tract of employment, for example dismissal, to be deal
with. Yet these are matters of vital concern to every em
ployee. How easily can he be declared 'redundant'? Is he
entitled to any compensation if he loses his job at shor
notice? Has he any appeal against dismissal on disciplinary
grounds? Trade unions may take up grievances on thi
score, and workers may strike if their grievances are no
met. But what is really needed here too is the rule of law -
the proper regulation of all these questions by agreement
No matter relating to the contract of employment should be
the exclusive prerogative of management.

Trade unions, as well as employers, are responsible fo
the failure of collective bargaining to reach its full develop
ment in this country. Their attention has been concen
trated on national and district agreements which deal with
wages and hours throughout the industry. But question
like individual job security can often be dealt with effec
tively only by works agreements, because circumstance
vary from one enterprise to another. It is here that collec
tive bargaining still falls short of its potentialities.

Industrial democracy undoubtedly depends on the fulle
development of collective bargaining, but it does not de
pend on that alone. Collective bargaining is primarily
method for regulating the contractual relations betwee
employers and employees; like the contract of employmen
it is a two-sided affair. But within each enterprise all th
various grades of employees are involved in other, many
sided relationships. They have to work together under th
same roof; they are subject to the discipline of the same man
agement. As a result, they are caught up in that who
complex of human and organizational relations whic
characterizes every tight-knit community. Here, too, th
abuse of power has to be checked and everyone given
chance to participate in the decisions which affect him
What form can democracy take in such a community?

Democracy in the Workshop

Having rejected workers' control, most trade unions have come to favour joint consultation as the method whereby democracy could be extended into the work community. During and since the war, there has been much talk about the need for joint consultation, but outside of the nationalized industries and a few, mainly large, private firms, it has not made much headway. Even where a whole hierarchy of consultative committees have been established, they do not seem noticeably to have changed the status of the workers or to have found much response from the workers themselves.

One of the difficulties in assessing the value of joint consultation lies in the uncertainty which surrounds its meaning. Unlike collective bargaining, it can mean almost anything. Representatives of management and workers consult together, but what do they consult about, and what are the results of their consultation? All that joint consultation does, of itself, is to provide a 'channel of communication'. The channel may be a very restricted one, and only a trickle may flow along it. Or quite a flow of information and opinion may be exchanged without appreciably influencing the actual decisions of management.

What joint consultation means in practice will depend on the purposes it is intended to serve, but these purposes are also far from clear. The supporters of joint consultation range from those who see it merely as a stepping stone to workers' control to those who, at the other extreme, believe that it could eventually make trade unions superfluous. The one predominant idea in most of the post-war propaganda for joint consultation – on the part of government, employers and trade unions alike – is that it stands and falls by the contribution it can make towards raising productivity.

Several variations are played on this theme. Sometimes consultation is regarded as a mere device for eliciting the workers' suggestions on how to increase output – a glorified substitute for a suggestions box. Alternatively it is seen as a means for strengthening their interest in the prosperity of the firm by taking them into the confidence of management – a cheap substitute for a profit-sharing scheme. There is, too, a more sophisticated view that it may help to diminish friction which might otherwise accompany technical innovation. According to any of these productivity conceptions of joint consultation, the workers are expected to accept unquestioningly the existing purposes of industry, although they show so little respect for their interests, and to cooperate with management in their furtherance. Is it surprising that workers do not display much enthusiasm when they are cast for so subservient a role?

This kind of joint consultation has nothing to do with industrial democracy. Rather might it be described as a change in the methods of industrial autocracy. In the past, management could rely mainly on fear and unthinking obedience for the exercise of its authority. All the way down the line superiors imposed their will on inferiors, with a 'yours-not-to-reason-why', and an unremitting pressure which had, as its final sanction, the threat of the sack. Full employment has undermined these old methods. As consent cannot so easily be enforced, it has to be won by persuasion. The emphasis shifts from punishments to rewards, or, in modern terminology, 'incentives'. The worker, if he cannot be bossed, must be manipulated. Intelligent managers have begun to appreciate that output can be increased by studying a man's happiness in his work; textbooks on 'human relations' become compulsory reading. The American trade unionists have found an apt name for this sort of study – 'cow sociology', or how to increase the milk yield by raising contented cows. The worker is human, yes. But because he is human, it is an insult to his dignity to be treated as the mere object of other people's subtle schemes.

No method of management deserves to be called democratic which fails to give every employee his full status as a human being. This is the crucial test. Once the simple assumption that every worker should be treated as a person not as an instrument, is accepted, then consultation is seen as a right. The claim to be consulted is a moral one which stands regardless of its economic result. There is every reason to believe that if a worker is consulted he will work with a better will, but higher productivity is the expected result, not the justification for taking his interests into account.

Consultation is a right, but what sort of consultation? It is not enough for workers merely to be asked their opinions so that management may take them into account, as it thinks fit. This may help management to gain consent for its policy; for the workers it is worthless. They are not interested simply in being consulted, but in being able to influence decisions. Only when they succeed in doing that are they likely to feel any responsibility for the outcome. The essence of democracy is active participation, not passive consent. The right to be consulted must mean the right to have a say. Anything less does more harm than good. By raising false hopes and then shattering them, the pretence of participation leads only to greater resentments.

How can consultation lead to responsible participation? The way is by no means easy, because the management of industry necessarily demands a clearly-defined structure of authority. Orders must be given and carried out, if any business is to be run successfully, or even to survive for long. This is why democracy in the workshop cannot take the form of majority rule; it would enable managers to evade responsibility by sheltering behind the anonymity of a majority vote. Management must retain full responsibility for another reason as well. It has obligations to those who work in the enterprise, but it also has obligations to the consumers of the products, and, within a framework of economic planning, to society as a whole.

The problem is to share managerial responsibility without abandoning it. Whether this is to be possible depends on three conditions. It depends, in the first place, on the actual structure of managerial authority. A democratic structure of authority, instead of being tall and narrow, is broad and flat. All decisions are not taken at some point at the top of a narrow hierarchy; they are decentralized and delegated outwards to the fullest possible extent. The greater the spread of authority, the more able is each level to secure the participation of those most affected by the decisions in their making. Every manager is then in a position to share his responsibility with his subordinates in the same way as he himself is invited to share responsibility with those above him. Unless the structure of authority is democratic in this sense, superiors are compelled to impose their will on inferiors. Each link in the chain finds himself enforcing on those beneath him decisions made by those above him in which he, too, has had no share. And the qualities demanded of him will be precisely those appropriate to authoritarian rule.

All managerial decisions cannot, of course, be brought within the immediate reach of every employee, not even if they are being taken at the level of authority with which he is immediately concerned – let alone the higher levels. There must be formal committee procedures for this purpose; this is the second condition on which responsible participation depends. What is required is a structure of representative committees paralleling the structure of management, so that all those subject to a particular level of authority may – at least through their representatives – be able to participate in the decisions taken at that point.

The third condition concerns the constitution and agenda of these committees. The work community is many-sided. There are not just two sets of interests, management and workers, to be reconciled, as in collective bargaining. All the various grades of employees – technicians, foremen, office staffs as well as the various groups of manual workers – have their own corporate interests. Each must be separately represented by delegates of its own choosing, who can voice the common concern of their constituents.* And the

* One of the familiar results of the two-sided production or consultative committees in some industries has been their effect on the foremen. Ground between the upper and nether millstones of superior managerial authority and the resistance of well-organized manual workers, their interests have been the most neglected and their position has become one of continual uncertainty.

delegates to be preferred are those who belong to a trade union and carry its backing; for without union organization to support them, their views may be given scant attention.

Although the representative committee at each level of authority will naturally be most concerned with the decisions taken there, no subjects – other than those which are dealt with by collective bargaining – should be arbitrarily excluded from any agenda. As soon as it is assumed that there is certain information with which the workers' representatives cannot be entrusted, or that certain decisions are the exclusive prerogative of management, co-operation on a basis of equality becomes impossible. The offer of second-class citizenship is as insulting in industry as it would be in politics. If trade secrets have to be safeguarded, this can be arranged by consent, just as defence secrets are safeguarded with the consent of Parliament.

These three conditions suggest a possible organizational framework for industrial democracy. They take for granted that workers want to participate in managerial decisions. But the familiar objection to any proposals for industrial democracy is that in fact workers have no such interest. True, the majority of employees to-day may show little concern for the export policy of their firm or its arrangements to purchase supplies of raw materials, although both may vitally affect their job security. But why? Perhaps they feel there is little point in being interested when they have no influence on what is done, and not even the information on which they could base a judgement. There are very few, however, who care nothing about the organization of their own work and the conditions immediately surrounding it. It is here that they particularly want to have their say, and, unless they do, they can hardly be expected to take much interest in anything else.

The realistic view is not that every worker wants equally to participate in every decision, but that many do want a voice in the decisions that directly affect them. The taking of these decisions is the growing-point of responsible participation. Even here not every worker will make use of his opportunities; not everyone is, or ever will be a committee man. For most, the practical, meaningful measure of industrial democracy will be how they are treated in their everyday work routine. But how they are treated will in fact depend on the influence their representatives can exert on managers and foremen at higher levels of authority. The nature of informal relations will be determined by the effectiveness of the formal relations which have been established. This is how democracy always works.

There is another objection advanced by the opponents of industrial democracy. The workers, they say, are all for claiming their rights, but are less willing to accept the responsibilities which go with them. The problem certainly exists; it is inherent in all forms of democracy. Rights and responsibilities go together; unless responsibilities are accepted, rights are endangered. On the other hand, no one can feel responsible if he is deprived of his rights; there is no reason why he should. Those who believe in democracy are prepared to accept its risks, because they know that the alternative – no rights and no responsibilities – is totally unacceptable.

A different kind of objection is raised by advocates of industrial democracy for whom consultation in any form seems inadequate. Effective control, they say, must rest on some final sanction. In politics this sanction is the vote; a government which does not satisfy can be voted out of office. But what is the sanction in industry? Supposing managers, in spite of all formal arrangements, nevertheless go their own way, what is to stop them? If, having gone through the gestures of consultation, they flout the agreement arrived at, what can their employees do? In fact, the worker has one final, unanswerable sanction; he can vote with his feet. He can control management with either an individual or a collective refusal to work. Given full employment and strong trade union organization, the workers certainly do not lack the power to insist on their rights.

Leadership not Legislation

Responsible participation in industry cannot be enforced by legislation. No matter what procedures are set up, no law can compel people to use them – let alone use them in the right spirit. In any case it is unlikely that a satisfactory law could be devised which would do justice to all the differing circumstances within the whole range of industry. This is not to say that legislation has no part at all to play. When, for example, the key industries were nationalized, the broad lines of their organizational structure were laid down in the Acts, and an obligation to institute arrangements for joint consultation was imposed. But the law cannot shape the internal organization and workings of industry. What happens in the workshop must depend on the actions of those who are directly involved.

How, then, can the democracy of responsible participation be advanced in industry? What we have already in the way of collective bargaining is primarily the result of many bitter trade union battles. The rôle of the unions is just as crucial in advancing democracy within the workshop. They are, after all, the representative organizations of that vast body of men and women who earn their living as employees. If they are content to use their strength only to drive up wages or to shorten hours, and pay little regard to the quality of the working lives of their members, then the existing institutions of collective bargaining are good enough. Workers may drive better bargains and still leave their status unchanged. Unless their own organizations claim a higher status for them, they are not likely to be given it as a present by their employers.

Trade unions to-day have all the power they need to fight this battle for an enlargement of the workers' rights and responsibilities. What they lack is the purpose. As they are democratic organizations, it is easy for the leadership to blame the members for their absence of interest, but that is a poor excuse. The job of leadership is to lead. The humiliation of being treated as an inferior rankles with many workers to-day, but for want of the leadership which only their unions can give, it usually finds a traditional expression in another wage-demand or in kicking over the traces in a seemingly pointless unofficial strike.

If the trade unions are to take up this battle, the emphasis in their activities now shifts from the council-chamber to the workshop. It is there where the main contests have to be fought. This highlights the rôle of the union workplace representative – the shop steward, or whatever other name he may be given. We have said that industrial democracy calls for decentralization of decision on the side of management; the same is true for the trade unions.

The relation between the unions and their workshop representatives – where they exist – has not always been a happy one in this country. Unofficial shop stewards movements and employers' attempts to use works committees in order to undermine union authority, have made trade unions reluctant, in the past, to give their shop stewards much scope. The wave of unofficial strikes since the war has not helped to diminish their anxieties. It is certainly not easy for the unions to control the activities of shop stewards in the same way as they can control the activities of their full-time officials, but the difficulties can be exaggerated. There is always the ultimate sanction of expulsion, when union policy is being defied, and to-day this may be a severe threat. The stewards would anyhow be less likely to join with unofficial movements if they felt that the union as a whole was conducting a militant struggle within the workshop. Often it is the failure of the unions to give a lead, or to take enough interest in what their stewards are doing, which causes them to look elsewhere for support.

The unions cannot possibly lay down in detail the policy to be pursued on every issue in every workshop, but they can decide many things in principle; for the rest they must depend on maintaining a close enough contact with the stewards. This is partly a question of organization, but it is even more one of education. A new type of working-class militant is needed – the man who can not only lead his fellow-workers in the struggle for their rights, but can also accept the obligations that go with them. Because the stewards ultimately represent their union and derive their strength from it, the union must accept the task of preparing them for this new, and in many ways far more difficult rôle.

Although trade union leadership could do so very much more, it cannot do everything. It is not within its power to alter the structure of managerial authority or to select and train managers for democratic management. Here management must give its own lead. There is, in fact, nothing to prevent management in private enterprise from pioneering new standards. From Robert Owen onwards it has happened occasionally in the past. To-day there are one or two firms with genuine experiments in industrial democracy which are certainly in advance of the nationalized industries. The mere fact that dividends have to be paid to shareholders does not compel managers to work on autocratic lines. The decline in the influence of the profit motive, even in private industry, has opened the way for change. It is part of the case for having a private sector that in it individual experiments are possible which might not have wider support.

Yet there is little hope that the generality of private enterprise will, of its own accord, do much to break new ground. Its managers are accountable only to the shareholders, and shareholders are not particularly concerned about the internal organization of the firm, providing their dividends are safe. Public enterprise, however, is in a different position. Here the government itself can pioneer. It can appoint or dismiss the supreme managerial authority; it can change the structure of management; it can insist on full consultation with the workers; it can, if only gradually, by selection and education develop a new type of manager who both wants and knows how to secure participation. And since the management of public enterprise is accountable to Parliament, Parliament can judge whether in fact new standards are being set. This should be regarded as one of the most important tasks of public enterprise.

There is yet a third possibility relating to private and public enterprise alike. Management might raise its own standards through the development of its professional associations. This has happened in other professions. In each of them a professional ethic has taken root over the years. Management, however, has as yet no such ethic of its own, no clearly defined standards of conduct. Indeed, there is not even agreement that management is a profession. Yet the power which managers possess over the lives and happiness of millions of people is certainly no less than that of the doctor or lawyer. Something more is required of the man who enters this calling than technical ability. It falls to managers themselves to assert their professional status and to set their own standards.

These three possibilities of democratizing industry are no more than possibilities. What trade unions demand, what society demands and what management demands of itself, all depend on the values they in turn hold. At present the values accepted by trade unions are not markedly dissimilar from those current in the rest of society; management, with its reputation to earn, readily falls into step. It is not that the superiority of the human values is denied, but they are regarded either as irrelevant to industry or incapable of realization.

This brings us face to face with the dilemma which lies at the heart of the problem of how to advance towards industrial democracy. Unless the workers do participate responsibly and influence the decisions of management, the purposes of industry and the way it conducts itself towards its employees are unlikely to be changed. On the other hand as long as the purposes remain what they are, there is no reason why the workers should want to participate in furthering them. To expect them to do so would be no more sensible than to expect a subject nation to co-operate in making a success of imperialism. Thus we seem to be caught up in a vicious circle of cause and effect, which allows pessimism on both sides to justify itself by pointing to its own barren results. Management can blame the workers for no waiting to accept responsibility, and the workers can blame management for denying them the rights without which responsibility would be a sham.

But vicious circles can be broken. They are broken by the few who refuse to accept the pessimistic assumptions that militate against change, and who demonstrate, in their own practice, how the impossible may yet be made possible. This is the very essence of leadership, and it is leadership of this kind – from the government in public enterprise, from management, and most of all from trade unions – which industry now requires. Against it all the forces of tradition, inertia, and cynicism stand arrayed.

PART THREE

A Socialist Economic System

11
THE ROOT OF THE MATTER

All the measures we have been discussing – whether for the advance towards economic security and fair shares, for an expanding economy, or for the introduction of industrial democracy – are at bottom concerned with one problem, how to bring economic power under social control. This problem has always been at the root of socialist thought.

What is meant by economic power? In any economy, no matter what its form, there are a variety of economic – or scarce – resources on which everyone depends for his livelihood. These include not only the three familiar factors of production – land, labour, and capital – but also the various forms of business organization and the whole mechanism of markets which knits the economy together. Those who have command of these resources possess economic power, by virtue of their being able to deprive others of access to them. The power of a landlord is evident when he refuses to allow his land to be used unless the rent he demands is paid. So is the power of a bank when it withholds credit, or of an employer when he dismisses employees, or of a trade union when it organizes a strike and withdraws the labour of its members.

In every economic system, someone commands the use of economic resources, and economic power is distributed among those who do. The power may be dispersed or concentrated. It may be in private or in public hands. It may be relatively unhampered or subject to all kinds of restraints. But however the economy is organized, some people take the leading decisions about the use of resources and therefore hold economic power. If they were left entirely free of control, the result would be chaos. The existence of an economic system means that the exercise of economic power is controlled, not haphazardly, because then there would be no system, but according to certain principles. What socialists have sought is a system, an organization of the economy, based on principles which would ensure that economic power was made to serve social ends.

12

OWNERSHIP AND POWER

Under the capitalist economic system which thrived in nineteenth-century Britain, economic power accumulated in the hands of the owners of capital, those who – in the familiar phrase – possessed 'the means of production, distribution and exchange'. They used their power for their own enrichment; it was curbed neither by legal regulation nor by social restraint. The only effective control to which they were subject was the invisible control of the market. They had to compete, and competition had a twofold effect; it compelled them to keep down prices, and spurred them to greater efficiency.

The guiding organizational principle of this system – at least in its pure form – was the maintenance of free and perfect markets. The state had no legitimate function within the economy except to uphold the rights of private property and to keep the markets free by preventing combination among employers and employees alike. The new 'dismal science' of economics was available to prove that the capitalists could do no wrong. The invisible controls of the market would lead them always in the paths of righteousness – assuming that nothing could be more righteous than increasing the wealth of nations.

Socialists challenged this system in two respects; they challenged both its ends and its means. They did not regard material progress as an adequate conception of the purposes which an economic system should serve – the injustice and conflict to which it gave rise were intolerable. They questioned too, whether a system subject, through its very lack of deliberate regulation, to periodic crises and to wasteful competition, was the best which could be devised even for the end of material progress.

Common Ownership as the Solution

The economic system which socialists envisaged was to be animated by quite different purposes. Its goal would be the common good, of which material progress was only one ingredient. To promote the common good, economic power had to be wrested from the capitalists and submitted to the visible controls of society, instead of to the invisible controls of the market. The simplest way of doing this, so it seemed, was to replace the private ownership of all property which represented power, by some form of common ownership. Then crisis and waste would be eliminated, an ever greater material progress secured, and its benefits shared equally among all.

But what was common ownership, and how could the transfer be brought about? It was these questions which sharply divided socialists into different schools of thought. They were agreed on the need to deprive the capitalists of their economic power, but they were by no means agreed on the precise ways by which this power would then be controlled.

For some, common ownership meant state ownership. Others feared that, if the capitalists were replaced by the state, the workers would continue to be exploited under a system of 'state capitalism'; they proposed alternative forms of social ownership. The advocates of a co-operative commonwealth visualized the gradual replacement of private enterprise by independent associations of producers or consumers organizing their own production or distribution on co-operative lines. The syndicalists believed that industry had to be captured from the capitalists by industrial unions – or perhaps by 'one big union' – which would then run it in the interests of the workers. The guild socialists took up an intermediate position between the state socialists and the syndicalists and favoured a partnership between the state and the unions, transformed into national guilds.

State socialists were themselves divided into two antagonistic camps, according to their views on how the transfer of power might best be accomplished. Revolutionary socialists advocated one all-embracing revolutionary act, by which the political power of the state and the economic power of the capitalists would be seized and held by a 'dictatorship of the proletariat'. Democratic socialists in contrast – and the British Labour Party has always been an intensely democratic party – were convinced that the change from private to public ownership must be effected by democratic methods, involving fair compensation and majority consent.

Yet in spite of these differing conceptions, common ownership was for a long time regarded as both an essential and an adequate condition for the establishment of a socialist economic system – not some common ownership, but complete common ownership of all the means of production, distribution, and exchange. In other words, the main emphasis in the socialist tradition has been on the transfer of economic power. Far less thought was given to its control. Not that the problem of control was entirely ignored. The assumption was, rather, that it would solve itself if only the transfer were made into the right hands – to co-operatives, to industrial unions, to national guilds, to a revolutionary or to a democratic state.

This assumption sprang from something more than blind faith; it was supported by the optimistic theories then current. Revolutionary socialists put their trust in Marxism. They were assured by this theory that, once the capitalists had been expropriated, economic classes would disappear and the state, which was merely an instrument of class rule, would 'wither away'. The 'dictatorship of the proletariat' would ultimately be replaced by a communist anarchy where no one would have the sort of power over his fellows which could be abused. Democratic socialists, on the other hand, were sustained by a theory of democracy which insisted that economic power could be effectively controlled by the vote. Whether the power of ownership were transferred to the state, or to the unions, or to both, or to any other representative organization of producers or consumers, the safeguard against its abuse would lie in the election of those who wielded the power, or at least of the authority to whom the power-holders were responsible.

These optimistic theories have now been shattered; socialists everywhere face the consequences. In the Soviet Union and, later, in other communist countries, Marxism has been taken to its logical conclusion. All economic power has been transferred to the state and the result is not a 'society of the free and equal' – as Marx believed – but a totalitarian tyranny. The state also commands all political power, and so is subject to no effective restraints at all. It is an even sorrier fate for the worker to be at the mercy of the state than to be the victim of private capitalists, for the state – unlike the capitalists – is ubiquitous. If capitalism is individualism run riot, then communism is collectivism run riot; the remedy is no better than the disease.

The advances towards common ownership in the democracies – and particularly in Britain under its post-war Labour Government – have also raised doubts about the efficacy of the usual methods of political democracy in controlling publicly-owned industry. There is no longer the confidence that a change in ownership is enough to ensure that an industry is run on socialist lines. Parliament may declare that nationalized industries must be administered in 'the public interest', and it may even try to specify what this means. But Parliament does not effectively control – and indeed it is often argued that it should not control – the internal working of the vast industrial organizations which it has created. Even with the support of powerful trade unions in all the nationalized industries, the individual employee continues to feel he has no real control over most of the circumstances of his working life. His vote, either as citizen or as a member of a trade union, is of value, but it is clearly not producing the results which were once anticipated. Discontent expresses itself in a waning enthusiasm for extending public enterprise in its present form.

The theories – whether revolutionary or democratic – which asserted that complete common ownership was the gateway to the promised land, no longer carry conviction

Because socialism has become identified exclusively with common ownership, loss of faith in common ownership as the great panacea often means loss of faith in socialism itself. There is an obvious way out of this dilemma if socialists have the courage to take it. The whole problem of ownership, and of how the power it confers can be socially controlled, must be examined afresh.

Changing Rights of Ownership

The case for complete common ownership rested on a number of mistaken conceptions. The first of these was the belief that the private ownership of capital was a bad thing in itself. One side of the coin of private ownership is undoubtedly power which can be abused. Yet, looking at the coin from the other side, private ownership can also be seen as a condition of freedom. Socialists have always recognized this when it came to personal possessions; only a few eccentrics have proposed to strip people of all their belongings. When the individual possesses nothing whatever of his own, he has precious little freedom of action, even in his most trivial personal affairs.

The ownership of business property is, of course, in a different category from personal belongings, but even here the problem of freedom arises. Once the state owns all capital resources, no one but the state is able to take decisions as to their disposal. Every business activity is subservient to the will of the government. There is no freedom to experiment with ideas which have not won state approval. The man who wishes to risk or dare is a misfit – or worse. To eliminate all private capital is to open the road to totalitarianism.

The second misconception lay in the belief that ownership was only dangerous in private hands. Once it had been transferred to public hands – so it was thought – the power it represented would be relatively harmless, for society would control it for social ends. Experience has now shown that the power of ownership, even in public hands, may still be dangerous. It is still open to abuse and the individual has still to struggle to assert his rights in face of it. Ways have to be found to control the powers of ownership, whether they are privately or publicly held.

The third, and perhaps most serious, misconception was the belief that ownership was one indivisible right, which could be held only as a whole – either by private persons or by public authorities; an industry was either wholly in private or in public control. In fact ownership consists of a bundle of rights. These rights are not sacred; they are upheld by the state and society. They are not fixed and unalterable; they can be changed and modified to any degree that state and society desires, and indeed they are constantly changing. Nor are they indivisible. Each separate right can be limited separately and by different methods; some can be in private and some in public hands.

Take, for example, the main rights associated with the ownership of business enterprise. There is the right to decide what is to be produced, the right to retain profits for personal use, the right to dispose of capital assets, the right to hire and fire. None of these rights are now absolute; each may be limited in one way or another. What is produced may be subject to direct government control, or, alternatively, to controls over the equipment or materials which the industry may use. Distributed profits may be curtailed by taxation, or by legislation to limit dividends. Capital transactions may be regulated. The engagement and dismissal of workers may be made to obey conditions agreed with the trade unions. Each right of ownership may in turn be circumscribed or transferred; indeed the rights of ownership can be invaded to such an extent that ownership no longer confers power. Little but the title – and the right to dispose of it – remains.

The twentieth century has witnessed how, step by step, the old unrestricted rights of ownership in regard to labour have been whittled away – through legislation, through trade union organization, through full employment – with the result that the power relationship between capital and labour to-day stands transformed, even when ownership s still in private hands. Indeed, in every respect, not only in regard to workers, we have seen how the rights of private ownership can be curtailed. The state can take over many of the rights of regulating production, distribution, profits, prices, capital transactions, and use them as it thinks fit. It has indeed gone further. By acquiring the ownership of basic industries, it has entered the market as a buyer and seller, so that it now has economic power of its own, as a counterbalance to private economic power. Yet other concentrations of power have developed in the hands of wholesalers or retailers or of the consumers themselves, which further limit the rights of the owners of industry. It is not unusual to hear the businessman, caught up in all these restrictions, complain 'I can no longer call my business my own', as indeed he cannot. Ownership no longer gives him the exclusive right to do what he pleases with what he owns.

Thus, although by far the greater part of British industry is still privately owned, we have a very different economic system from that which existed a generation ago. What has been achieved is due not to the abolition of private ownership, but to all the various controls by which the rights of ownership have, piecemeal, been limited. The growth of these controls reflects, too, some change in the purposes which the economic system is expected to fulfil. Society is no longer content that the sole end should be the pursuit of material progress, at no matter what social cost. It has begun to insist that the benefits of material progress should be more evenly spread among all sections of the people, and that economic power should be harnessed in the interests of some broader social good.

Market and Managerial Power

In spite of all these changes, ownership remains the source from which economic power is ultimately derived. It is ownership which, in the final analysis, gives people the right to dispose of scarce resources, and therefore to deny other people access to them.* How is it, then, that although the rights of ownership have been so drastically curtailed, economic power itself has not in any way lessened? On the contrary, we are more conscious than ever of great concentrations of economic power – public and private – which are able to dominate the lives of producers and consumers, and of the community at large.

The reason for this lies in the growth of organization within the economy. Not only has the scale of business enterprise increased, but with it the size and influence of economic associations of all kinds. The distribution of economic power has been affected in two important ways. It has, first, been concentrated and enhanced. Individual owners have pooled their rights to dispose of their resources, and the concentration of power which has resulted exceeds the sum of its parts. The bargaining power of a trade union, for example, is far greater than the total of the individual bargaining power of each of its members; the same is true of the power of a joint-stock company or of any other large business organization. And second, the actual command over the use of resources is separated increasingly from their ownership and transferred to managers or officials. The real power-holders to-day are those who exercise authority within these organizations and take decisions on their behalf – the leading directors and executives. While still deriving from the rights of ownership, economic power is exercised less and less by the owners themselves.

The major concentrations of economic power to-day take two forms. There is, first, the power of those who command the supply and demand of goods and services in any of the various markets in which buying and selling, lending and borrowing, hiring and firing take place; this may be described as market power. The holders of market power are rarely the owners of the resources which they command. They are the managers of large-scale business enterprise

* There is the special case of the scarce resource – labour. The individual worker, if he is free to dispose of his own labour, is here regarded as its owner.

who direct all the firm's market operations. They are the banks which command the supply of currency and bank credit, without being the owners of the funds they handle. They are the insurance companies and building societies which command, but do not own, the savings of millions of owners, many of whom previously had nothing to save. They are trade associations and marketing boards controlling the supply of anything from raw materials to finished products. The workers have also built up a considerable market power of their own. They have trade unions which command the supply of labour, and co-operative societies which command the purchasing power of their millions of members. Finally, there is the state itself, operating in almost every market, controlling the supply and demand of resources of all kinds.

The second form of power is within the business enterprise. Firms have become larger in scale, more complex in function, drawing their mounting capital funds from a host of different shareholders, and the owners have found it necessary to entrust their conduct to expert managers. These men, whether in private or public enterprise, exercise managerial power within the internal organization of each separate business. They may be regarded as the representatives of the owners, but their power derives from something more than the collection of buildings and machines which comprise the assets of the concern. Each enterprise is an organization, with a structure of authority, accumulated experience, and good-will; the power of managers exists by virtue of this organization. An enterprise may pass from private to public hands, so that a radical change in ownership is effected. But the organization may remain untouched; even the same people may exercise managerial power after the change as before.

Both market and managerial power arise from ownership but are enhanced by organization. In both cases the power is exercised by those at the head of the organization, rather than by the many separate owners. The distinction is in the place where power is exercised. Market power is exercised in the markets – the commodity markets, the labour markets, the money markets. Managerial power is exercised within the internal organization of business enterprise. Industrial management in fact wields both; it operates within a framework of markets, and at the same time it controls the internal conduct of its firm. This, in essence, is the 'managerial revolution' which has gone so far to divorce the exercise of economic power from ownership and thus transformed the problems of social control. The real importance of the distinction between market and managerial power lies not in their separation, but in the different ways by which they can be controlled.

13

THE CONTROL OF POWER

Control by Checks and Balances

One way of controlling economic power is by counter economic power. We see this happening in every market. Two sides meet to strike a bargain; their interests conflict. Each seller uses his power to exact as high a price as possible for his product; each buyer uses his power to minimize the price. The lender of money wants a high rate of interest, the borrower a low. The workers claim a high wage for their labour, the employer's concern is to buy labour as cheaply as he can. Each naturally tries to push his own advantage. Neither can have things entirely his own way, but the one with the greater power will get the best of the bargain; he will be the privileged party.

For socialists, there is no reason why either side should be privileged. When private interests clash in a market, neither is necessarily to be preferred; neither should be possessed of the superior power which would enable it to impose its will on the other. Yet it is impossible to divide power between everyone in exactly equal parcels. Even if this could be done in the Utopia of which anarchists have dreamed, no sooner will power have been so divided than those who were more energetic or thrifty or cunning, would begin to increase their holdings at the expense of others. This idea of an individual sharing-out is anyhow totally unrealistic in the markets of to-day which are dominated not by individuals but by massive organizations representing sectional interests.

What is possible to aim at, instead, is a balance of power between contending forces. The power of sellers, in each particular market, might be roughly balanced by the power of buyers; the power of lenders by the power of borrowers; the power of employers by the power of trade unions. Whenever a conflict arises, the power of each interest will be controlled by the balancing power of the other. Neither side will be able permanently to dominate; to reach agreement each must respect the other's wishes. The socialist principle according to which economic power should be distributed between the two parties to any market transaction might be described as the principle of the balance of power.

How is such a balance to be attained? There is a natural urge among the victims of superior power to take what action they can in self-defence. We have seen this happen under capitalism. In its heyday economic power was confined almost exclusively to the propertied classes. Competition among themselves held them, to some extent, in check, but there was little to prevent the abuse of their power over the propertyless. This situation spurred the workers into action. They organized themselves into trade unions and co-operatives to create power of their own, and they succeeded at least in curbing the unbridled power of the capitalists.

This is a continuous process in the markets; wherever one party dominates and the other is free to defend itself, sooner or later it will try to do so. Such voluntary action is always to be preferred to state action; it is better for people to take care of their own interests than to rely on others to do it for them. Here is the essence of the case for collective bargaining rather than state regulation of wages and working conditions, for consumers' co-operatives rather than government price-fixing. But voluntary action alone, however determined, will not always do the trick. There is no internal mechanism within the economy, brought into play by the promptings of self-interest, which can guarantee a fair division of power. Even when trade unions had come into being, the workers remained the weaker party. They were forced to turn to politics for further help, and it was from the state that the necessary assistance came.

State intervention is usually needed to establish a balance of power between rival interests because all economic power is upheld by law. To change its distribution, voluntary action must ultimately be supported by legislative action. The power of a property-owner, for instance, exists because the law safeguards his property from theft and invasion; by changing the law his power can be curtailed or transferred into other hands. Even the power of trade unions has a legal basis; it could not exist without the legal right for unions to use their funds as they wish, to bargain and to strike. Economic power of every kind is upheld by legislation; its redistribution therefore demands government action.

The nature of this form of government action is, then, to alter the distribution of economic power in order to establish a balance between conflicting private interests. The distribution of power cannot be determined once and for all in a free society. Changes are constantly occurring as new resources or new forms of association are developed. Each new situation calls for fresh government action. It is only in a completely stagnant economy that the pattern can be finally set.

Control by Strategic Participation

Even if the balance of power were adjusted to meet every situation, it would do no more than minimize the abuse of power by either party to a transaction. At best this is a negative control; any economic system with positive purposes to fulfil would require something more. Economic power has to be purposefully directed towards social ends. There must be some overall guidance of the economy. This can only come from the state. In other words, the control of economic power by counter economic power does not suffice; there must be political control as well.

Political control of the uses of market power is commonly known as economic planning. There is, of course, nothing inherently socialist about planning – it may just as soon be capitalist or fascist or communist. Everyone is a planner now; there is practically no country and no government which is prepared to throw itself unreservedly on the mercies of unregulated markets. The mere fact that planning takes place tells us little. Every government claims to plan 'in the public interest' or for 'the common good', but these are labels which can be stuck on any jar; it is the jam inside that counts. 'Planning,' in the words of Professor Tawney, 'like parliaments and public education, is not a simple category. Its results depend . . . on the purposes it is designed to serve, the methods which it employs in order to realize them, and the spirit which determines the choice of both.'*

Socialist planning has its own definite and distinctive purpose. Its object is to maintain a framework of opportunities – opportunities as secure as possible, as equal as possible and as large as possible – in which each individual can shape his own life. Put more concretely, socialist planning aims at achieving economic security, fair shares and an expanding economy. As soon as the government intervenes beyond the provision of this framework of opportunities and begins to decide how they are to be used, it invades personal freedoms and violates the values on which socialism rests. What a man makes of his opportunities is his own affair, as long as he does not use them to harm others. He wants the chance to work in a suitable job, but he does not want to be forced into any particular occupation. He wants the chance to live securely in reasonable comfort, but he does not want to be told where to live or how to spend his income. He wants to enjoy many and varied amenities, but he does not want to have his leisure pursuits settled for him.

This means that a socialist economy is not just a planned economy, but a planned market economy. It is through the markets that individuals exercise their freedom of choice. If workers are to be free to choose whether to work for one employer rather than another, and employers to choose which workers to employ, there must be a labour market. If consumers are to decide whether and on what they want to spend their money, there must be commodity market in which they can make their choice.

* R. H. Tawney, *The Attack*, 1953, p. 95

What of the methods of planning? There are two very different paths which can be followed. The first is to leave economic power in private hands and attempt through legislation, or through administrative controls, to regulate the decisions of the power-holders. This is 'control from without'. The second method is for the government to enter the economy, by itself taking possession of economic power. Through its own participation within the economy, it then exercises 'control from within'.

All democratic planning involves some measure of 'control from without'. In an economy where economic power is not totally in public hands, the government is bound to resort to this form of regulation. But its disadvantages are well known. Legislation is an inflexible and clumsy method for dealing with a dynamic economy. It can cope only with general and permanent problems. For this reason administrative controls, which can be used to impose specific and temporary restrictions have been preferred. But these, too, have their dangers. Even if arbitrariness and corruption are avoided, a division of responsibilities is created which clearly leads to inefficiency and frustration. In a word, administrative controls run into all the problems of 'bureaucracy'. What is more, they can only restrict, not innovate. Economic planning has been discredited among freedom-loving people because it has been associated too closely with 'control from without'.

Socialist economic planning must rest primarily on the alternative method of 'control from within'. Here the government legislates to acquire economic power of its own, thus bringing the decisions regarding its use into the direct orbit of political control. In this way it can act positively; it can pursue its own objectives, not merely prevent others from acting contrary to them. To do so it need not invade the whole economy and seize total economic power; it need occupy no more than the strategic positions. From these key points, it can permeate and direct, even though considerable power still remains in independent possession.

The strategic position from which the government is able to exercise 'control from within' over the use of financial resources is the budget. Through the budget it raises revenues and decides how they are to be spent. If the aim is economic security, the government can regulate the total flow of money, so that it is sufficient to sustain demand and maintain full employment, but is not so much as to cause inflation. If the aim is fair shares, it can alter the distribution of incomes by taxation and by the provision of various social incomes. If the aim is an expanding economy, the government can determine the division of the national income between consumption, investment, and social expenditure so as to serve this end. Thus, in countries where people pay their taxes, there is much to be said for the view that of all planning instruments the budget is 'the most important, the most powerful and the most embracing.'*

Yet where economic power rests on the command of physical – not financial – resources, the budget loses its effectiveness. Something more is required. Planning for economic security, for instance, involves the continual adjustment of demand and supply; but whereas the budget can control normal changes in demand, it cannot directly control supply, nor does supply adjust itself automatically when the changes in demand are too rapid or drastic. Some planning of production is also needed. The government may itself have to enter the economy as an investor. Similarly, the budget has limits in planning for fair shares. Taxation may reduce the differences in incomes, but inequalities have also to be tackled at their source by the government taking possession of the big accumulations of property. Again, in planning for an expanding economy, the budget may ensure that the nation's savings are adequate, but it cannot curb the bad effects on output both of monopoly and excessive competition. Public enterprise, at strategic points in the market, is needed for this.

In the past, socialists have tended to underestimate what

* W. Arthur Lewis, *The Principles of Economic Planning*, 1949, p. 27.

ould be done by the budget. Because all governments have a budget to raise revenue, its potentialities as an instrument of planning were underrated. But now a new danger has risen – the danger of thinking that the budget can do everything. Yet its limits are as obvious as its possibilities. The state can control the use of financial resources through the budget, but not the use of physical resources. Socialist planning demands both. The strategic use of the budget has therefore to be supplemented by the strategic use of public property.

The principle by which economic power is directed towards socialist ends may be described as the principle of planning through strategic participation. The state takes over economic power at the key points in the economy – the budget, the key industries, large property concentrations – and uses these as its planning base. How the government uses its planning powers and what it plans for, will always be under public scrutiny, for in a democracy, the state itself is controlled by Parliament and all the normal political processes.*

But political processes alone are not a complete safeguard. They are remote from the daily scene of economic operations, and do not always prove effective in detailed application. This is the significance of limiting the government to no more than a partial participation in the economy. As long as an independent sector remains, it can act as a perpetual and very effective check on the state's activities. If there continue to be private employers and independent trade unions, and bargaining between them produces good results, there will be no escaping the insistence of the unions on similar conditions from public employers. If public enterprise is less efficient than private, if it gives less satisfactory service to the consumer, the comparison will be

* We would guard here against the impression that, in a democracy, any government can plan in isolation and then impose its will. Many interests have to be consulted, not only through Parliament, and their co-operation won before any plan has a chance of success. And in the execution of the plan, decentralization is most important.

there for all to see and public opinion will not acquiesce for long. If private investment meets the nation's needs, there will be no call for public investment. At every point the nature and efficacy of state activity can be directly challenged.

Control by Social Accountability

The principles of the balance of power and of strategic participation relate to the control of market power. Neither of these principles – nor both together – is adequate to deal with the problems posed by the concentration of managerial power. Each may influence the use of managerial power, but neither is fully effective in directing it towards socialist ends. The economic control exercised by competitors in the market may stimulate managerial efficiency, but competition is never more than an imperfect check; inefficient firms survive with a surprising tenacity. The countervailing power of trade unions can press managers to pay high wages, to improve the conditions of work, even to alter the processes of work. But these are all pressures from outside; they cannot change the very structure and methods of management or bring about the adoption of new purposes in industry.

Political control has similar weaknesses. The government may take possession of an industry, appoint its managers and give them directions. But no government can know what is going on within each of thousands of enterprises supervise their internal running and take responsibility for all that is done. It cannot lay down by law how people are to treat each other or how they are to behave, and little will be gained by hamstringing management with paper regulations which cannot be enforced. Even were all these things possible, what of the businesses that are not publicly owned? What control would there be over the power of their managers, except perhaps the example of the better run public enterprises?

There is a third method of controlling economic power

control by society itself. Society here means not only a vague and general public opinion, but those groups in society who are most affected by managerial power, are in a position to know how it is exercised, and are able to make their influence felt. Such a specific social control can be a potent force. In politics, the power of the vital organs of public opinion is unquestioned, even in matters not likely to overthrow a government. The knowledge that society – or the influential groups within it – will refuse to tolerate certain actions is a strong deterrent to most politicians; and when society insists that certain things shall be done, sooner or later it will have its way.

Social control cannot operate in an organizational vacuum. Socialists have had reason to be suspicious of those who relied on reform merely through a change of heart and the preaching of moral values. They have always insisted on a change in economic organization as well. The organizational form of social control is social accountability. Three conditions are needed to render it effective. The first is that those who exercise power must be made directly accountable to those who are concerned with the way their power is exercised. The second condition is that social accountability must be backed by sanctions; there must be some ultimate means by which those who fail can be brought to book. The third is that what is asked of those who hold power must be known. There must be clearly defined standards for their conduct. If the standards are not formulated, it cannot be asked that they be respected.

The machinery of accountability can be developed in various ways. In co-operative organizations managers are made directly accountable to their members – this is an essential feature of their democratic structure. In public enterprise, management is ultimately accountable to Parliament. But Parliament is remote, and in private enterprise it exercises no control at all over the conduct of managers. Both in public and in private enterprise a more specific accountability is called for. On the consumers' side there are many devices, ranging from the Consumers' Council to the prevention of misleading advertisement. On the producers' side, there is accountability to the workers themselves through the machinery of industrial democracy. In each case powerful sanctions can be brought to bear. The individual consumer can refuse to buy, the individual producer can refuse to work. And just as the government can come to the support of the consumer, so can the trade unions come to the support of the worker.

But what of the crucial third condition – clarity on the standards by which managerial performance is to be judged? In the past the standard was plain enough. A manager stood or fell by the profit and loss account he presented at the end of the year; as long as business was good, how he used his power within the enterprise was a matter of small concern. This simple standard has now become shaky and discredited. Even in private enterprise profit is no longer accepted as the sole measure of good management.

Instead a new standard is replacing the old one; profit is being replaced by productivity. Even the case for public enterprise is argued mainly on these grounds; co-ordination, efficiency, control of monopolies, improved industrial relations are all seen as means for increasing output. To suggest that public enterprise might provide the great opportunity for applying socialist ideals, with their respect for the individual, to the actual running of industry, is to invite dismissal as a hopelessly impractical idealist. A business enterprise, we are told, exists to produce goods and services and must therefore justify its existence only by its success in the market. What effect it has on the lives of people who work in it is irrelevant.

Yet the standard that socialists should now be upholding, and which should be applied wherever managers give account of their stewardship, is precisely this – that socialist ideals be applied to the conduct of industry, both as regards man as consumer and man as producer. Managerial power has always to do justice to the duality of the effects of economic activity on the life of man. Of course efficiency is desirable, but the rights of man as producer deserve no less attention. This, too, should be a criterion by which society judges the exercise of managerial power.

*

These three guiding principles for the control of economic power – the principle of the balance of power, the principle of planning through strategic participation, and the principle of social accountability – form an integrated whole. They draw together the threads of our present argument, so that out of the warp of the ends and the weft of the means the pattern of a socialist economic system can be woven. It is an economy with a private and a public sector, but where all economic power, no matter what its nature or by whom it is held, can be made subject to effective control. This control may be economic, political, or social. Each of these forms may be applied separately or in combination.

This conception has nothing in common with that misleading picture of a faultless and unchanging set of economic institutions which we rejected at the outset. Socialist ideals can never be expressed in terms of an institutional Utopia, for institutions are never perfect. They must continually be adapted to new conditions. What we have done is to state the principles of organization which should underlie the choice of institutions. The way these principles are interpreted, the institutional framework which is in fact chosen, lends itself to infinite variety. That should surprise no one, for the circumstances which have to be met are themselves infinitely variable.

Conclusion

14
LOOKING TO THE FUTURE

Any political creed, if it is to survive, must be both an inspiration and a guide to action. Socialism is no exception. It cannot live on old loyalties or on the record of past achievements. It must arouse devotion among the present generation, and prove its relevance by showing them too how to act. Unless it continues to generate heat and light – heat in the hearts and light in the minds of men – it will lose its appeal and end in the limbo of history.

Maturity in movements, as well as in people, brings dangers which youth can afford to ignore. Ideals that when untried, were bright with promise, shine dimly, if they shine at all, when the difficulties in the way of their realization have been revealed. At the same time, as the arteries harden there is less willingness to look around with fresh eyes and adjust methods realistically to new conditions. The readiness to challenge outmoded ways is often replaced by a fixed attachment to them; the heresy of yesterday becomes the orthodoxy of to-day. Waning idealism as regard the ends and growing dogmatism in the choice of means are the twin dangers of advancing years.

The demand for the rethinking of socialism, which has come to the fore in recent years, reflects an awareness of these dangers. The British labour movement has never allowed itself to become the slave of doctrine. It may be slow to adjust its traditional policies, but it will do so when convinced of the need. That conviction has been gaining ground. The Welfare State has still to be defended against indirect attacks, but socialists know that a defensive battle is no longer enough. They are reaching out for the new objectives and the new methods of advance. The essence of our argument is that these objectives will only emerge when the idealism has been restored to our ends; and the practical next steps will only be defined by seeking a new realism in the choice of means.

Equality and Beyond

The hard core of socialist idealism has always been the concept of equality. The repudiation of class, the demand for fair shares in the distribution of the good things of life, the longing for a society in which people, no longer divided by the barriers of privilege, can be conscious of their common humanity – everything that is really distinctive in socialism as a political movement springs ultimately from this source.

Equality can, of course, be given a narrow interpretation and applied only to the distribution of material things – incomes, property, the money spent on education or other social services. For understandable reasons, equality in this sense has been the first preoccupation of socialists. Their first task was to iron out the intolerable disparities which divided society into two distinct nations – the rich and the poor.

But if socialists are to continue to think only in material terms, theirs will be a limited appeal. They will distinguish themselves from their opponents only on how what is produced should be distributed. This is not a difference to be ignored, because the divergencies in income and property and educational provision are still conspicuous enough to stir a social protest. But the goal of material equality is no longer sufficient to inspire a generation which has all the jobs it wants, and more money in its pockets to spend on pleasure than its parents had to live on for weeks. This is no longer a cause capable of evoking the dedicated idealism of an earlier era.

The ideal of equality has now to be given a more meaningful expression. Socialists have always spoken about equality of opportunity, but this only raises the further question 'opportunity for what?' We can hardly be indifferent to the kind of opportunities which are offered – whether they are to express one's own personality in one's own way or merely to keep up with the Jones's, whether they are to help one's neighbour or to get the better of him, whether they are to have a job one likes or simply to have any job at all. There must be some standards to which a society aspires, and by which the opportunities it provides are judged. What socialists value are all those opportunities which enable people to live in freedom and fellowship, which enrich the content of life and put the quality into equality. To ignore these ideals, to consider equality in isolation from them, is to open ourselves to the charge that socialists have no care for individuality and the graciousness of life, but are concerned only with a mechanical sharing out of what is.

On the other hand, the acceptance of these ideals takes us far beyond equality. To divide opportunities – even of an ennobling kind – fairly, is not enough. We want also to enlarge them; to open up an ever-widening range of outlets for self-expression and service. These new horizons, with their yet untasted freedoms and yet untried responsibilities, might stir the pulses of a rising generation in a way that material betterment alone has signally failed to do. Socialist idealism confined to a wholly materialist strait-jacket is – under present conditions – crippled from the start.

Within this strait-jacket, only two questions are relevant to economic life – 'how much is produced?' and 'how is it distributed?' These are in fact the questions on which socialists have concentrated. But once the strait-jacket is discarded, two further questions immediately call for a reply – 'what is produced?' and 'how is it produced?' These are the neglected questions of our time. Their neglect accounts for the topsy-turvydom in our production priorities, which puts washing-machines and refrigerators before houses, cars before roads, and commercial television before schools. It accounts too, for bad relations in industry, for the failure of many workers to find an interest in their work for their indifference and their cynicism.

This unconcern with the questions 'What?' and 'How?' does not mean that people deny the values which lie behind them and believe that man can live by bread alone. What they deny is their relevance to economic life. Talk of freedom and fellowship is considered fine on Sundays, but what has it to do with the weekly chores of earning a living? No one challenges the ideals in the abstract; they only prove with the devastating logic of 'what is must always be' or 'human nature being what it is', how impossible such ideals are of attainment in the economy – which is, after all, a very important segment of our common social life.

Yet the questions of 'what is produced?' and 'how is it produced?' are far from foreign to the socialist tradition. They were being posed – and posed forcefully – before they were overlaid by the practical tasks of tackling poverty and unemployment. Now they can and must be recalled to life, for they epitomize the full breadth of the socialist vision.

The Private Sector

The keynote of socialist realism has always been its emphasis on a transformation of the economic system. This must remain. What has to be rejected is the idea of transformation through total public ownership; that leads only to totalitarianism. The first part of realism to-day is to recognize this fact and accept its consequences. A socialist economy is a mixed economy, part private part public, and mixed in all its aspects. It comprises private spending as well as public spending, private ownership as well as public ownership, private enterprise as well as public enterprise.

In practice this is already accepted by the British labour movement, but the doctrine of total public ownership has confused thought. Socialists seem to talk one way and act another, with a schizophrenia that has upset themselves, bewildered their friends and played into the hands of their enemies. It has enabled unscrupulous opponents to depict socialism as a stage on the way to communism itself. Socialism becomes identified with the all-powerful state, with heavy-handed bureaucracy, with regimentation and rationing and other unpleasantnesses.

The private sector of a socialist economy is not there merely on sufferance, to be tolerated only on grounds of political expediency, with the Sword of Damocles hanging over it in perpetual threat. On the contrary, it has a legitimate and indeed a necessary function to perform. Within the limits of equality, there must be opportunities for people to spend as they wish, to own, to initiate and experiment; they must be able to form associations to further their economic interests. In all these arenas, the individual must have a chance to act without waiting for the approval of the state.

If this is to be the important function of the private sector, then it cannot be hamstrung by a whole network of legislative and administrative restrictions. That would only defeat its purpose. The method of controlling activities in the private sector should rather be by the maintenance of a balance of power in the markets, so that conflicting interests are given equal weight. Government intervention is required, not to deprive people of their right to take decisions and accept responsibilities, but to alter the distribution of power so that the balance is maintained and no private interest is privileged.

In their uncertainty about the rôle and permanence of the private sector, socialists have given relatively little thought to their policy for dealing with it. True, a balance of power has been established where it was once most desperately needed – between the large opposing interests in the labour market. Strong trade union organization and full employment now enable trade unions to negotiate on equal terms with employers. But between the well-organized workers and employers on the one hand, and the producing and trading monopolies on the other, what happens to the ultimate consumer, and to the small producer or tradesman? The balance of power is weighted always in their disfavour. Consumers' free choice often amounts to little more than a 'take it or leave it'. And for the man who wishes to stand alone, to do things his own way, there is little protection. He is stifled by the overwhelming resources of the combines against whom he must compete.

To see that the balance is restored here as well, is as much a part of socialism as anything else. Deliberate government action is demanded to give the consumer and the small man the protection to which he is entitled. There are many ways of doing this, ranging from the regulation of restrictive practices or the introduction of government wholesaling, to such comparatively simple measures as consumers' advice or easier credits for the small manufacturer or trader. The reason why a socialist economy requires a private sector is because socialists place a value on individual freedom. Their duty then is to ensure that freedom is in fact maintained within it – not crushed out of existence by the empire builders of the market.

The Public Sector

The public sector has an entirely different role. Whatever decisions are taken in the private sector are determined by private interests; the social outcome is a matter of chance. Once the idea is discarded that there is a self-adjusting mechanism in the markets which will always work for the good of all, the case for a public sector is established. The government must step in where individuals or private organizations are bound to fail, because of their lack of will or lack of capacity. If there is to be any certainty of achieving our ends, some overall planning of the uses of the nation's resources is essential. Planning, through outside controls though sometimes necessary, may be both dangerous and ineffective. The socialist way of planning is by the direct participation of the government at the strategic points of the economy; in other words, there must be a public sector through which to plan.

Where realism falls short to-day is in thinking of the public sector almost exclusively in terms of nationalized industries. That is an error deriving from the days when all economic power was identified with the ownership of the means of production. But economic power, we recognize now, may take many forms, and the public sector includes all forms of economic power which are under the direct control of the state. The budget itself is an important part of the public sector; it gives the government control over the expenditure of vast revenues, which may be used to serve social purposes. The public sector includes, too, public ownership and public enterprise in many guises. It is not only industries that may be publicly owned, but property of all kinds – land, buildings, shares in business concerns. And enterprise itself covers so much more than large-scale basic industries; it can equally take the form of a new town, or a municipal restaurant.

As soon as one considers the ends of socialism, the limitations of our present public sector are evident. We need more public expenditure, more public ownership, more public enterprise. Not that there is virtue in any of these for themselves, but for the purposes they may be made to serve. There is no virtue in the government spending more money, unless it spends it on developing all those community needs and services which private spending will never provide. There is no virtue in property being owned publicly rather than privately, unless the government takes possession of the large concentrations of property in order to advance towards fair shares. There is no virtue in public enterprise in itself, but it is essential if the government is to plan for economic security and an expanding economy. What is needed is not just more and more of any of these, but more to be used towards clearly defined ends. The first question is never 'how much?' but 'what for?'

Yet 'how much?' is the question that is constantly being asked. As if any one could tell in advance the precise, mathematical proportion of the economy which must be publicly owned before 'socialism' has arrived! A doctor may as soon foretell how many spoonfuls of medicine the patient must take before he is 'cured', or the teacher how many books his pupil must read before he is 'educated'.

The question puts the cart before the horse. If socialists would stick to the real issue – 'what for?' – 'how much?' would take care of itself.

The Limits of Legislation

There is yet another part of realism – to recognize the limits to what can be done through legislation. Socialists have put too much faith in a telling legislative programme. Yet, in all that concerns the internal conduct of business enterprise the arm of the law is very short. Managers can only be properly controlled in the exercise of their power if they are made socially accountable for its use. It is here that socialist action has fallen most conspicuously short. Except for a few isolated experiments, the idea of making managers accountable to their workers is still an alien thought; nor would there be agreement as to how to go about it. We are still groping for ways for protecting the consumer. Even in the case of the public industries we do not know how to achieve accountability to Parliament in any effective sense; indeed we are not entirely sure whether we want this to happen.

Difficult as it is to develop the machinery of social accountability, the machinery by itself will not take us very far. How it is used depends on the standards set for the conduct of enterprise, and leadership alone can change these standards. This is where the managerial and technical professions have an important function. If socialists refuse to concern themselves with these professions, and regard managers only as implacable enemies, they will not get very far in changing the conduct of industry.

But the role of the trade unions is even more important, because the rights of man as producer are recognized least of all. Unless the unions insist on a change, it will not come about. Their members are those most affected, with the most direct power to insist that their demands are met. One of the most important tasks in the advance towards a socialist economic system falls, in effect, not to politicians and constituency parties, but to trade union leaders and works committees.

That attitude which asserts that the industrial wing is more a handicap than a help (except, of course, for the money it provides) and that socialism would be achieved sooner without it, is utterly unrealistic. It is based on twin misconceptions – that socialism has little to do with the life of man as producer, and that it can be brought about by legislation alone. The truth is that we have only arrived where we have through the combination of political and industrial action in the past; it will require the same combination to take us where we want in the future.

The Will for Change

The rethinking of socialism is a necessary preliminary. But thinking alone will not effect social change; there must be a will for it. The destination may be clear, the paths leading towards it well-defined, but will people care to make the journey? Here we are confronted with what is, probably, the deepest source of defeatism among many life-long socialists to-day. They doubt whether the will for socialism still exists, or whether it can be created anew in this modern age of material comforts. Perhaps the majority of people are now content with what they have, or even if not content, perhaps they are concerned with no more than raising their own standards of living. There is certainly no noticeable urge to embark on new social experiments which may exact some toll in the form of higher taxes or new responsibilities, or some sacrifice in overcoming the inertia of established practice. Are we indulging in an illusion if we believe that anything very different from the present Welfare State can ever find substantial support among the people? Maybe socialism has foundered on the political paradox that nothing fails like success.

We do not share these pessimistic doubts. We believe that man aspires to something more than economic security, more even than the new luxuries which additional income might provide. But people are conditioned by the accepted values of their times, which so many of the existing institutions tend only to perpetuate. The very growth of the techniques of mass communication, brought about by man's increasing mastery over nature, strengthens the influence of these institutions. Almost without exception, they feed the illusion that what is, is good, and more of what is, is better. The struggle to change accepted values thus transcends the bounds of politics and economics; the whole culture of society is involved. The socialist David who would attack this Goliath has no stone in his sling other than his own conviction that man is capable of, and worthy of, a mode of living fine far beyond his present experience.

One David alone cannot win this battle. We need an army of his like in every walk of life. He is every active member of the Labour Party, who recognizes his individual responsibility for its future. He is the trade unionist who seeks something more than the pay-packet, and the co-operator who looks beyond the dividend. He is the shop-steward or the manager who defies conventions in order to bring a new spirit into industry. He is the teacher with a new conception of the meaning of education, the welfare worker who refuses to capitulate before the plight of the unfortunate. Not least, he is the artist, the architect, the writer, the poet, who can make us acutely conscious of human potentialities. He is every rebel whose integrity will not allow him to conform.

These, in all their different ways, are the standard-bearers of the new society. Whatever else has changed, one thing Keir Hardie said half a century ago has lost nothing of its relevance:

> *If anything is to be really done in this world it must be done by visionaries, by men who see the future, and make the future because they see it.*

Some other Penguin Specials
and relevant Pelican books
are described on the
remaining pages

THE HOUSE OF COMMONS AT WORK

Eric Taylor

The author is Clerk to the Committee of Privileges of the House
of Commons. He has written an account of the daily workings
of the House at the present time – its procedure, rules, committees, and methods of dealing with proposed legislation.
(A257)

LOCAL GOVERNMENT IN
ENGLAND AND WALES

W. Eric Jackson

A simplified explanation of what the Local Government system
is, its place in the national scheme, and the numerous important public services which various types of local council perform.
The citizen, the student, and even the member or official of a
local authority, will all find it useful as a companion for brief
and easy reference. (A162)

THE ENGLISH PARLIAMENT

K. R. Mackenzie

A survey of the historical development of Parliament describ-
ing how and why it has come to work in the way it does to-day.
The Spectator commented: 'Mr Mackenzie has done an altogether admirable piece of work, covering ground which has
never been covered in so succinct a form, which badly needed
to be covered and which is covered here as effectively as could
be hoped for.' (A208)

SPOTLIGHT ON ASIA

Guy Wint

The clash of rival traditions and philosophies in Asia

s164

Mr Nehru often urges people in the West to recognize how fast Asia is changing. But the change has not begun only in our day. It started with the British occupation of India which transformed the sub-continent. India became the home of a liberal civilization, and in course of time its political institutions have become those of parliamentary democracy. Besides India, the other great originating centre of civilization in Asia is China. In China there has also been radical change, but the result has been to create a civilization derived partly from the example of Communist Russia and partly from the traditions of Asia's despotic past. Voluntarily or involuntarily, India and China are now in competition to see which is to become the pattern for the rest of Asia, and the issue is complicated by the world struggle of the great powers.

This book records these vicissitudes of the Asian continent, and describes a competition on whose result much of future world history will depend. For, as Lenin said, 'In the last analysis, the issue will be determined by the fact that Russia, India, and China represent a crushing majority of the population of the globe.'

A PENGUIN SPECIAL

COMMUNISM AND CHRISTIANITY

Martin D'Arcy

s163

Communism has been called a religion, and in so far as it has a creed which is wholeheartedly believed the name is not unjustified. What the Apostles' Creed is for Christianity, the Communist Manifesto is to its followers, a call to belief and action. Both creeds claim to give an answer to the chief problems which agitate man – his individual and social life, his origin and destiny.

The aim of this book is to compare their answers, to examine their validity, and to see how far they are at variance and where, if at any place, they come together. The writings of Marx are first studied in their historical setting and in relation to the place of the individual in society. An account is then given of the development of Communism and of the influence of Lenin and Stalin upon it. Communism has always claimed to be a revolutionary system dependent upon a few simple and fundamental ideas. These ideas are examined and then contrasted with the principal tenets of Christian philosophy, which has had a formative influence on the culture of the West and which touches the same concerns and problems as its Communist rival. The last part of the book deals with this Christian philosophy of man against the background of the Communist view of human life. The Christian view is exposed not so much in its strictly religious teaching as in its cultural value and its claim to truth.

A PENGUIN   SPECIAL

OUR LANGUAGE

Simeon Potter

A227

Can we ever know too much about the words we use every day of our lives? It is the purpose of Dr Potter's book to present a clear and up-to-date picture of the English language as it is spoken and written in all its variety and complexity. Dr Potter believes that more people to-day are interested in speech than ever before and that a new spirit of linguistic enterprise and adventure is astir. All of us are becoming more conscious of our mother tongue as something living and changing and amenable to our corporate will. The story of our language is one of gain and loss. Its peculiar structure and its superabundant vocabulary are the outcome of long centuries of growth. To-day, English is both strong and rich but, even at its best, it is far from perfect. Is it beyond the wit of man to remedy manifest deficiencies in its inherited mechanism? Can we make the English language of to-morrow yet more effective as a means of communication? These, and scores of other similar questions, will readily occur to the intelligent reader.

'The author is brilliantly successful in his effort to instruct by delighting . . . He contrives not only to give a history of English, but also to talk at his ease on rhyming, slang, names, spelling reform, American English, and much else. The book is admirably clear in its main outlines, but its interest for the common reader derives from the wealth of examples at every point: the chapter on names is particularly well done. Altogether a fascinating book.'—*Higher Education Journal*

RELIGION AND THE RISE OF CAPITALISM

R. H. Tawney

A23

Religion and the Rise of Capitalism is a study of religious thought on social issues during the three centuries from the later Middle Ages to the early eighteenth century. Starting with an account of medieval theories of social ethics, it goes on to examine the impact on traditional doctrines of the new forces released by the economic and political changes of the age of the Reformation. The social backgrounds and teaching of Luther, Calvin, and the English divines from Latimer to Laud receive attention in turn. A chapter on the Puritan Movement discusses, among other topics, the theory that Capitalism had Puritanism as one of its parents. The conclusion reached by the author at the end of his survey is that 'the criticism which dismisses the concern of Churches with economic relations and social organization as a modern innovation finds little support in past history. What requires explanation is not the view that these matters are part of the province of religion, but the view that they are not.' While the book is primarily concerned with changes in the world of thought, it is not confined to them. Holding that theories, in order to be understood, must be read in the light of the practical realities which help to produce them, it devotes part of its space to a consideration of the latter. It attempts to explain the conditions which gave point to prohibitions of usury and to the insistence on a just price; describes the social consequences of the Tudor land question; and touches on the impetus to economic speculation given by the price-revolution, the expansion of foreign commerce, and the growth of the money-market.

THE PELICAN PHILOSOPHY SERIES

General Editor: A. J. Ayer
*Grote Professor of the Philosophy of Mind and Logic in the
University of London*

Aquinas – *F. C. Copleston*
An introduction to the medieval philosopher whose influence
is great in the thought of to-day (A349)

Berkeley – *G. J. Warnock*
An introduction to the writings of the eighteenth-century Irish
philosopher (A286)

Ethics – *P. H. Nowell-Smith*
A classification of the words and concepts in daily use and the
connexions between them (A293)

Hobbes – *Richard Peters*
An account of the seventeenth-century thinker who covered
most fields of philosophy and religion (A367)

Kant – *S. Körner*
A new introduction to the philosophy of one of the greatest
thinkers of the modern world (A338)

Leibniz – *Ruth Lydia Saw*
One of the great seventeenth-century intellectuals whose new
system of philosophy is explained (A305)

John Locke – *D. J. O'Connor*
A critical introduction to the seventeenth-century empiricist
who founded the British philosophical tradition (A267)

John Stuart Mill – *Karl Britton*
An introduction to the teaching of this famous nineteenth-
century political philosopher (A274)

Peirce and Pragmatism – *W. B. Gallie*
An explanation of the theories of the great nineteenth-century
American philosopher (A254)

Spinoza – *Stuart Hampshire*
A general introduction to the work of the seventeenth-century
Dutch philosopher (A253)

The Vocabulary of Politics – *T. D. Weldon*
An inquiry into the use and abuse of language in the making of
political theories (A278)